PRESERVES

JILL NICE

PRESERVES

A BEGINNER'S GUIDE TO

MAKING JAMS & JELLIES, CHUTNEYS & PICKLES, SAUCES & KETCHUPS, SYRUPS & ALCOHOLIC SIPS

JILL NICE

Collins

For my willing 'tasters': David, Ben, Lotte, Lucy,
Steve, Vivien, Nick, Jessie, Ols and the B.B.

First published in 2011 by Collins

HarperCollins Publishers
77–85 Fulham Palace Road
London W6 8JB

www.harpercollins.co.uk

15 14 13 12 11
9 8 7 6 5 4 3 2 1

A catalogue record for this book is available from the British Library.

ISBN: 978-0-00-742079-7

Designed by Lucinda Lowe

Printed and bound in China by South China Printing Company Ltd.

CONTENTS

INTRO

UCTION

Preserving is an ancient method of extending the keeping qualities of a wide variety of ingredients. Traditionally used to make the most of a glut of seasonal produce, it is still very popular today and potting up and preserving delicious surplus foods has become a creative, worthwhile and sometimes even profitable hobby.

Preserving has a considerably different motivation nowadays than in the past, when the desire to put food by, whilst it was available in quantity, was a driving force and could literally mean the difference between life and death. Today, our desire to preserve food is to provide better choices for our families, to ensure the food we eat is pure, wholesome and unadulterated, to make the best possible use of local and freshly grown produce and to make the most of the best available ingredients. There is also, of course, the undoubted facts that your own preserves will taste superior and give you much more value for money than if you opt for the shop-bought variety.

I often hear people say how they think making jam is so time-consuming, so here I've made the quantities easily manageable and the methods as simple as possible. There is no longer the need to pot up tons of fruit and vegetables to see us through the bleak months of winter – the availability of produce throughout the year and the ability to store food in fridges and freezers has changed all that.

Making your own preserves has become more a desire to experiment and produce the unusual and different, to offer up exciting choices for the table and to make exotic presents for your friends and family – who could

resist homemade Peaches in Brandy Wine (page 184–5) or Cranberry and Kumquat Pickle (page 129–30)? There is also the possibility of all the wonderful tarts, pies and puddings filled with your own creations, those mouthwatering mixtures of apples, pears and plums; rhubarb jam, preserves of gooseberry and apricot with names redolent of the countryside – September Jam (page 139), High Derry Down Conserve (page 187–8) and Blackberry and Raspberry Jelly (page 118–20).

The cold table has never looked so appetising either – jars of pickled and spiced fruits and vegetables add sparkle to a platter of cold meats and salads. Rich and flavourful chutneys boost homemade crusty bread with a good cheese; spicy sauces and jellies complement tasty pâtés or pies, to say nothing of perking up a plate of bangers and mash.

Preserving all this natural bounty brings out the most ancient of our squirrelling instincts, to put by today what we may not have tomorrow. However, unlike the squirrel, we do not have to search for our hidden bounty beneath a tree, but can gaze upon shelves of glowing and colourful pots and feel eminently pleased with ourselves and the fruits of our labours.

THE DIFFERENT TYPES OF PRESERVES

So, you've decided on the main ingredient, but what should you make? And just what is the difference between a jam and a conserve or a chutney and a pickle?

JAM

In its simplest form, jam is fruit boiled with sugar to prolong its keeping quality and prevent it from going mouldy. The effect of heat releases the pectin (see page 34) and acid, present to some degree in all fruit, which then combines with the sugar to form a set. Jam should be a relatively smooth amalgam of fruit and sugar, most usually used for spreading on bread, toast or cakes. In the United States, jam is often referred to as jelly or spread. Jams such as Greengage and Red Gooseberry (page 153–4) or Green Tomato Jam with Limes (page 94–5) are quite unique.

CONSERVES JAM

Also sometimes referred to simply as preserves, these are
pieces of whole fruit suspended in a jellified syrup, for example
Cassandra's Gooseberry Conserve (page 145), the truly exotic
Fresh Fig Preserve with Sherry (page 140–1) or Strawberry Conserve
(page 217). These are quite delicious and unique and are often eaten as
a dessert with cream or used as a filling for sweet flans. Victoria Plum
Preserve (page 195) and Quince and Parsnip Preserve (page 202–3) are
also utterly delicious and can only be made by your own fair hand.

CURDS

These are usually made from citrus fruits, particularly lemon, in which
the pulp, peel and juice are combined with eggs, sugar and butter to
give a rich, thick mixture (see page 157 for an Old-Fashioned Lemon
Curd recipe). Lemon curd is a wonderful treat, but without artificial
preservatives it does not last well, so make a small quantity and keep
it in the fridge. Other fruit, such as raspberries, gooseberries, apricots
and peaches, can also be used by substituting 450g fresh fruit, puréed,
for the lemon.

CHUTNEYS

A combination of fresh and dried fruit and/or vegetables, hot spices,
herbs, sugar and vinegar mixed together to make a chunky mixture in
which no flavour predominates. They can range from sweet and mild
to ferociously spicy. Chutney should be soft and slightly runny when
cooked – the mixture thickens and improves in flavour when kept. In
India, the land of its origin, chutney was made with uncooked ingredients
and brought to the table raw. Nowadays, it is more usual to set it aside to
be eaten at a later date with cold meats and bread and cheese.

Chutney is an excellent way in which to use up gluts of fruit and veg,
such as windfall apples, plums, marrows or green tomatoes, that are

sometimes less than perfect and correspondingly cheaper or, if you're really lucky, even free! Tomato Chutney (page 96) or Hot Rhubarb Chutney (page 211) make use of glut produce and last throughout the winter to make a good addition to sandwiches and salads.

RELISHES

Relishes are a soft amalgam of fruit and/or vegetables, such as Red Pepper Relish (page 90). These delicious goodies are not as long-lasting as chutneys, but they can be made reasonably quickly and are an extremely useful addition to the ubiquitous barbecue menu. Because they spread easily, they are also excellent in sandwiches. Make small pots or keep in the fridge once opened. Hamburgers and sausages will be perked up with the Celery and Tomato Relish (pages 59–60) or Chilli Relish (page 61–2).

PICKLES

There are three types of pickle. One in which the amount of vinegar used is proportionately lower than the quantity of fruit and sugar, therefore a spicy 'set' pickle is achieved. The second type is where fruit and vegetables are partly cooked in a spicy vinegar. The last variety of pickle is made by preparing vegetables in a salt or brine mixture and then packing them into jars of well seasoned vinegar or sauce, for example Pickled Onions (page 84) or Hot and Spicy Pickled Red Cabbage (pages 57–8). Homemade pickles are so much better than commercially produced pickles – no additives, no artificial preservatives – just a wholesome fresh flavour and you can have lots of fun experimenting and even more enjoyment out of the eating!

A pickle like Spiced Gooseberry Pickle (page 147–8) can be made throughout the year and adds a welcome boost to a cold supper.

SPICED FRUITS AND FRUITS IN ALCOHOL

Spiced fruits are dried or fresh fruit that have been carefully brought to the boil in a well-spiced vinegar, simmered and then transferred to a jar. The vinegar is then boiled to reduce it, strained and poured, while it is still hot, over the fruit. My favourite fruits to use are Hunza dried apricots (see Spiced Apricots, page 114–15), prunes and mixed dried fruit. After having been left for a month to mature, they make a very welcome appearance at a festive table.

Alcoholic lovelies are fresh fruit, for example, peaches or greengages, which are gently poached and placed into a jar, covered with syrup and topped up quite extravagantly with alcohol. See Peaches in Brandy Wine (page 184–5), Vivien's Grapes in Muscat (page 151), your own pear liqueur (page 190), Sloe Gin (page 213) and Blackcurrant Shrub (page 132).

SAUCES AND KETCHUPS

A preserved sauce is the thick, runny reduction of fruit and/or vegetables cooked with vinegar, sugar and spices; it is then sieved before being bottled. These sauces are most often used as flavourings in soups, sauces and stews. Tomato and Brown Spicy are the most familiar shop-bought sauces. There are some marvellous mixtures, which are very economical to make and last ages. Traditional ketchup (not at all like the popular tomato variety) was at one time a pungent mixture of spices, onions, garlic, occasionally mushrooms and berries, which were allowed to macerate in vinegar for a good length of time before being sieved and bottled. Worcestershire Sauce is the most similar commercial product to a traditional ketchup. Homemade sauces bear no relation to commercial varieties – Spicy Fruit Sauce (page 197) is a welcome addition to the table, whilst Mushroom Ketchup (page 75–6) perks up stews and casseroles.

THE KEY INGREDIENTS USED IN PRESERVING

FRUIT & VEGETABLES

FRESH FRUIT AND VEGETABLES

Thanks to the miracles of modern science and improvements in transport, most fruit and vegetables are available throughout the year. However, in the cause of economy and being environmentally friendly, it is far better to buy your fruit and veg from local markets or shops that you know source produce grown within an acceptable distance or, if you can, grow your own. Also, make the most of farm shops and pick-your-own farms. Another good local source to keep your eyes open for are glut fruits and vegetables, which are offered by gardeners rather than see them go to waste. These are often excellent buys or they may even give them away – try a bit of bartering!

If you've chosen a recipe that includes exotic fruits that aren't grown in this country, then do buy them in their natural season and from as close by as possible. Always wash them well to ensure that any wax or preservative coating is removed.

For detailed information on specific types of fruit and veg, refer to the recipe section.

STORECUPBOARD FRUIT AND VEGETABLES

Apart from being able to treat your family to pure, unadulterated and imaginative preserves, the reason for making these good things is to take advantage of fruit and vegetables when they are fresh, in season and when they should be correspondingly cheaper. During the winter months this is not always an option, therefore a little cheating may be necessary...

TINNED FRUIT AND VEG

These make exceptionally good preserves. Measure off the juice and use it with, or substituted for, the liquid in the recipe. If it is sweetened, reduce the sugar by 1 tablespoonful per tin. Gooseberries, apricots, plums, pineapple and tomatoes are the most successful. Tinned sweetcorn can be used in relish to cheer up the ubiquitous hamburger.

FROZEN FRUIT

Look for bargains at your local pick-your-own farm shop (many have freezers full of fruit) or check out your local supermarket for offers – frozen fruit, particularly berries, can sometimes be cheaper than fresh.

DRIED FRUIT AND VEG

Dried fruits are essential for chutneys and pickles, but there are a host of jam and conserve recipes that make good use of dried fruit during the winter months. Dried tomatoes and mushrooms can be used in pickles and chutneys.

FRUIT JUICES

Good-quality, preservative-free, pure fruit juice can be a useful standby for jellies and to add to other fruit.

SUGAR

White sugar is produced either from sugar cane grown in the tropical regions of the world or from sugar beet, which is produced in more temperate climates. Although there is no difference between the two, my preference has always been for cane sugar.

Sugar, like honey, wine and spices, was used in early kitchens in order to disguise, or improve upon, mediocre and stale food and was considered to be a costly and exotic spice. Only the well-to-do and wealthy in Britain could afford to use sugar as a preservative and it took hundreds of years for it to become the everyday commodity that it is now. Sugar acts as a preservative only when it is used in conjunction with a pectin and/or acid.

Jams and jellies with an inadequate amount of sugar will inevitably give poor results. You may have to over-boil the jam to compensate for the lack of sugar and this will not only give a bad colour and taste, but the preserve will not thicken or set properly. The preserve will probably not keep and it may not be entirely fermented (an easily recognisable condition in which the preserve tastes like wine); or it may taste sour or grow an unappetising mould. Jams and jellies with too much sugar will be oversweet and lacking in flavour. They will also crystallise during cooking or whilst the preserve is being stored.

The proportions of sugar to fruit are very important and recipes should be followed in this respect, but for those who would like to go it alone, here are some rough guidelines, but remember that the fruit must always be fresh and unbruised (see page 34 for the pectin content of different fruits):

1kg high-pectin fruit requires up to 1.25kg sugar

1kg medium-pectin fruit requires 1kg sugar

1kg low-pectin fruit requires approximately 800g sugar

Certain important steps to be taken with sugar will ensure a clear, bright jelly or jam with a good set and, hopefully, no problems afterwards. Always warm the sugar in a heatproof dish in a very low oven (70°C/gas mark ¼) for 10 minutes before adding it to the pan of fruit or juice; this will not only keep the colour good, but also help the sugar to dissolve more rapidly. The sugar must be thoroughly stirred in and dissolved before the preserve is brought to the boil – if you do not do this, you will find that you have crystals forming in the jam or, worse still, it will sink to the bottom of the pan, stick and burn and there really is no salvaging that little error! This applies to chutneys, pickles and sauces as well as to sweet preserves.

Do not boil for longer than you have to once the sugar has been added. Unless stated otherwise, the boiling should be as rapid as possible to prevent the fruit skins hardening in reaction to the sugar and to keep a good, bright colour and fresh flavour.

Do not stir too much or leave the spoon in the pan once the sugar has been added and brought to the boil – it may make it more difficult to achieve a set. Take care not to boil past the point of setting – it's worth remembering to remove the pan from the heat as you test for a set, otherwise it may well just bubble past the setting point whilst your back is turned.

Lots of different types of sugars are available. Here are the advantages, or otherwise, of each:

PRESERVING SUGAR

A white sugar that has larger crystals than granulated sugar and creates less 'scum' (for want of a better word). It therefore requires less skimming and ensures a brighter, clearer jam or jelly, although it would be wasted on chutneys.

JAM SUGAR

A white sugar that has added pectin and is very useful for making preserves from fruit with a low pectin content. Strawberries, rhubarb and raspberries can be very temperamental, as can plums and apricots, and dried fruit certainly needs extra help. Jam sugar is not necessary when making preserves other than jams or jellies.

WHITE OR GOLDEN GRANULATED SUGAR

White granulated sugar is most commonly used in preserving as it has no colour or distinctive taste. It is cheaper than preserving and jam sugar, but does not dissolve so easily and often forms a scum, which will impair the appearance of jams and jellies, although not the taste. If this happens skim the scum off before potting. Golden granulated sugar gives a slightly mellower flavour and, when used in light-coloured preserves, a richer colour. However, golden granulated sugar is more expensive than white, and I can see no real advantage in using it.

WHITE CASTER SUGAR

This is more expensive than granulated sugar, but is necessary in some exotic recipes and for making curds. If you do not have caster sugar, then whizz some granulated sugar around in a blender for a second or two.

LIGHT BROWN SUGAR, SOFT BROWN SUGAR AND DEMERARA SUGAR

These are made from sugar cane and are less refined than white sugar. All of these sugars can be used in preserves, but as they do not usually form a set when used alone, they should be used in conjunction with white sugar. Whilst many people believe that using brown sugar in their preserves has a beneficial effect, I find that it impairs a satisfactory set, therefore it is better used in those preserves in which a firm set is not essential. When using high-pectin fruit such as apples, gooseberries and damsons, a reasonable set may be achieved by substituting half or a quarter of the white sugar for brown, but low-pectin fruit such as apricots, peaches and strawberries will not achieve a firm set without the use of additional pectin, and it is as well to remember that brown sugars will alter both the colour and the taste of the preserve, so it is best to use them with strong, dark fruit, for example damsons and plums.

Light brown, soft brown and Demerara sugars can give additional colour and taste to fruit cheeses, chutneys (where they can be used very satisfactorily in conjunction with brown malt vinegar), relishes and sauces. Once again, as in all preserves, do make sure that the sugar is dissolved before bringing to the boil.

SOFT DARK BROWN SUGAR, MUSCOVADO, MOLASSES AND BARBADOS SUGAR

Very dark, rich sugars that will flavour and colour quite strongly. Unless a recipe specifically advocates the use of any of these sugars, they should only be used in chutneys and sauces.

ICING SUGAR

Unsuitable for use in preserving.

All of the following can be substituted, in part, for sugar:

GOLDEN SYRUP

A refined by-product of white sugar, which gives a lovely taste to preserves and a golden colour to pickles. It also fractionally changes the consistency. Golden syrup is best used by substituting a quarter of the sugar for syrup, preferably in preserves made from high-pectin fruit such as apples or gooseberries, where it adds a golden colour. The same proportions can be used when making syrups for spiced and alcoholic fruit. Always warm the tin before measuring and pouring – it makes life so much easier.

BLACK TREACLE

Thick, dark brown supremely sticky stuff. Used only sparingly to give a strong flavour and dark colour. Very few jams use treacle in the ingredients, but it is occasionally useful in chutneys, etc.

CORN AND MAPLE SYRUP

These are most popular as accompaniments to waffles, pancakes and fritters, but can also be used in preserves. Substitute a quarter to half of the white sugar for syrup and remember that both dark corn syrup and maple syrup colour quite distinctively and that maple syrup has a strong taste.

HONEY

Absolutely delicious in preserves. It is much sweeter than sugar and has a unique 'wild quality' that it imparts to any preserve in which it is used. Mixed blossom honey is the most economical choice, but there are some wonderfully flavoured pure blossom honeys: clover, eucalyptus, rosemary, orange blossom, heather and lime. Do be careful to blend blossom honey carefully with the fruit in the preserves because their tastes are quite distinctive. I would not recommend using chestnut blossom honey in preserves as it is very overwhelming. I like to use the more delicately flavoured honey for use in fruit curds, where it can transform the flavour. Honey added to jam makes it a subtly different preserve, but it will not set if used alone, therefore substitute a quarter to half of the sugar for honey depending on the fruit or flowers used and the consistency of the set preferred.

MOLASSES

Very thick and black and not suitable for use in home preserving.

SALT

Salt is particularly important in the making of chutneys and pickles for many reasons. Strong brine acts as a preservative and prevents the process of discolouration if used with care. Salt sprinkled on such vegetables as cucumbers rids them of excess moisture and helps to soften hard skin. Salt also removes bitter juices from fruit and vegetables such as aubergines and prevents juices from leaching into the vinegar. Salt gives a unique pungency to lemons and limes, which is totally unlike their natural flavour; it also combines with herbs and spices to give magical effects from the most basic ingredients.

Some recipes require a lot of salt and some very little, and I would suggest that you stick to the quantities given. Remember, that when reducing pulps, purées and pastes, the salt flavour will become more concentrated.

Never neglect the addition of salt in your recipes, unless you are on a salt-free diet, in which case it is worth investigating salt substitutes. Salt brings out the flavour in food that might otherwise be dull and lifeless. This strange property is why fortunes have been made, and the prosperity of nations founded, upon salt – you do not realise how vital it is until you are deprived of it, and then a terrible craving sets in! Apart from which, it was at one time the only method of preserving foodstuffs – from fish and meat to fruit and vegetables.

Salt should be kept in non-porous stoneware jars or wooden boxes and a few grains of rice added to ensure that it stays dry and free-flowing – especially if you keep salt near the cooker. Damp salt becomes concentrated and can cause mayhem for the careful cook.

Several varieties of salts are available:

TABLE SALT

The most widely used type, table salt contains magnesium carbonate to give it free running properties, but I feel that this makes it unsuitable for clear pickles and bottling as it may give a cloudy result.

ROCK SALT

A crystal form of salt, this is the next best thing to block salt, which was traditionally widely used in preserving but is now difficult to obtain.

BAY SALT, SEA SALT OR GROS SEL

These are crystals of sea water formed by evaporation under natural or artificial heat. This is the salt that I find most satisfactory for nearly all preserving.

MALDON SALT

Flat flakes of salt naturally produced in Maldon in Essex. Maldon salt is the very best, but also the most expensive.

FLAVOURED SALT

Ready-made celery salt, garlic salt and onion salt are all popular kitchen condiments and each adds their own distinctive flavour to a wide variety of dishes. But how about making your own herb salts? Take a bunch of fresh mixed herbs, choosing a selection that is suitable for a specific purpose. For example, use the more delicate herbs like chervil and tarragon in creamy sauces; robust herbs like marjoram and sage will go well with meat and fish; whilst strong, aromatic herbs such as oregano and basil are the most suitable for pizzas and cheese dishes. Make sure that the herbs are freshly picked, clean and dry and chop them finely. Either put them into a liquidiser or mix very thoroughly by hand in a bowl or pestle and mortar with three-quarters of a cup of an additive-free salt. Spread the mixture out thinly on a baking tray and leave overnight in the oven at a very low temperature (50–70°C/gas mark ¼), with the door ajar. Store in an airtight container – the herb salt will last indefinitely, but all herbs lose their flavour over time.

VINEGAR

An essential ingredient in a wide variety of pickles, chutneys and relishes, not only to add colour and flavour, but also to prevent the growth of bacteria and so extend the keeping qualities of the finished preserve.

Choosing the right vinegar can be a daunting prospect as the range available at supermarkets is ever-increasing, so here's a guide to the different types:

MALT VINEGAR

Made from a fermentation of malt, it is available as either brown (coloured with caramel) or white (distilled). This vinegar is the one that most home preservers favour, for it is economical, can be purchased in large quantities from 1–5 litres and is easily available. However, do make sure that the vinegar you purchase is true malt vinegar. Although malt vinegar is harsh and uncompromising, it is quite suitable for more robust pickles, chutneys and sauces where refined flavours would be lost. White malt vinegar is usually used in conjunction with white sugar, where a light, clear or decorative appearance is necessary, for example artichoke pickles. Small green tomatoes, red chillies, shallot or pickling onions, pieces of lemon and so on will show to better advantage if white vinegar is used.

WINE VINEGAR

This was originally made from wine in Orléans, France, where great casks of stored wine suffered from the accidental inclusion of air, thus becoming disastrously soured over a period of time. Eventually, the value of this unpalatable wine was discovered, financial disaster was averted and a more scientific approach was worked out for making Orléans wine vinegar. Many companies now make less expensive wine vinegar by modern methods. Wine vinegar is better than malt vinegar in delicate pickles (if there is such a thing!) but do not be misled into thinking that because it has a more fragrant flavour it must be better for pickles, for this is not necessarily so. Wine vinegar has a different effect on some combinations of fruit, vegetables, spices, etc, and may result in a sour note. One of the best uses it may be put to is in herb vinegars (see page 27).

CIDER VINEGAR

This is produced in much the same way as wine vinegar. It can vary enormously in quality and price and the flavour can be pleasant and mellow. It is much more useful in nearly all preserves than wine vinegar and is, if you can afford it, a better substitute for malt vinegar, especially if you favour natural foods. If you run out of cider vinegar in an emergency, half white malt vinegar and half dry cider will give you a reasonable result and this is the mixture that I frequently use in preserves that are well cooked. Cider vinegar is excellent for making flower, fruit and herb vinegars (see page 27), although it does have a clear golden colour that you may consider to be a disadvantage.

BALSAMIC AND SHERRY VINEGARS

Powerful, dark vinegars most usually added in small quantities to sauces, dressings and other dishes. Too strong to use in pickling – and the cost would be prohibitive – however, in conjunction with malt vinegar, they make a well-flavoured pickling vinegar for shallots and mushrooms. A good slug of it will also give a kick to red tomato chutneys and sauces.

SPICED OR PICKLING VINEGARS

Many recipes call for this ready-spiced vinegar and it is handy to make it in large quantities, which can save a lot of hassle later on. Most of them are made from malt vinegar, although occasionally a recipe may specify a spiced wine or cider vinegar. The method of making spiced vinegar is simple: pickling spices are boiled together with vinegar in a stainless steel pan, the pan is removed from the heat, covered and left to get cold. It can then either be strained before using or the whole spices added to the pickle, but not to a chutney. If it is to be kept, it should be poured into a suitable container and sealed with a non-metal lid. The spices added to the vinegar will make it much stronger if you don't strain it. A wide selection of different spiced vinegars, both mild and fiery, are included throughout this book.

FLAVOURED VINEGARS

There are many recipes for malt vinegars flavoured with garlic, onion, shallot and horseradish; white malt vinegar flavoured with cucumber; wine vinegar with tiny red chillies or green peppercorns added to the bottle; and, of course, the vinegars left over from such goodies as pickled artichokes or onions. All of these are of inestimable value in the kitchen. A few drops added to salad dressings, marinades, stuffing, dips, chutneys and pickles all give your own special, unique touch and, of course, are very economical and will give a zing to the most everyday food.

HERB VINEGARS

Most of these are usually made with white malt, red or white wine or cider vinegar, and there are many recipes in this book for achieving these delightful and subtle concoctions. Use attractive bottles for a never-ending supply of unusual and inexpensive presents, which will give great pleasure to you and the recipient. The most exciting thing about making herb vinegars is the experimenting. Do not just take the recipes that I have given, try mixing and blending your own favourites. How about several coriander seeds with lemon thyme for a spicy vinegar or a few cloves or a blade of mace in a tarragon vinegar? This makes a smashing dressing for chicken salad. The therapeutic effects of wandering around the garden selecting your herbs and then going through the leisurely business of preparing the vinegar and waiting for it to mature are very good for the soul as well as the palate.

Although there are more specific recipes, there is a fairly standard method of making herb vinegars. Use only small quantities of herbs to start with and try experimenting with your favourites, adding a few whole spices if the mood takes you. If it is difficult to obtain fresh herbs, then dried herbs will still make a very palatable vinegar. Generally speaking, half the weight of dried herbs to fresh is sufficient, but remember when using dried herbs to strain the vinegar through a muslin cloth before decanting otherwise it will be 'bitty'. Make sure that you pick your herbs before they flower and early in the morning whilst their oils are still fresh; also, that they are clean and dry – but do not wash them. Bruise them well and pack into a sterilised heatproof jar. Bring a pan of white vinegar to the boil and then pour it over the herbs whilst it is hot, but not boiling, then seal and leave to infuse for 14 days, shaking every day. Strain and add a fresh whole leaf or a sprightly sprig to a sterilised bottle before adding the vinegar. Seal with corks.

FLOWER VINEGARS

If making herb vinegars is soothing, imagine the delightful pleasures in store in making fragrant vinegars, perfumed and colourful with names from an Elizabethan garden – gillyflowers, clove carnation, rose, lavender and marigold. White vinegars are used to make these ancient lovelies as the vinegar becomes transformed by the colour of the petals. One word of warning though: do not use flowers grown from a corm or bulb base unless you are absolutely sure that they are not harmful. It is also good common sense to check on any flower that you use to make sure it is not one of the nasties.

FRUIT VINEGARS

More old-fashioned brews concocted by good wives of another era and some of my favourites. Again, use white malt, cider or red or white wine vinegar and usually soft fruit: blackberries, raspberries, mulberries or blackcurrants. The results can be put not only to culinary use, but to medicinal use as well. With hot water and honey added if necessary, children will find them a soothing and novel antidote for minor snuffles and sore throats. Inevitably the originality is half the cure!

SPICES & FLAVOURINGS

Without a pinch of spice or a grating of ginger, many preserves would simply not be as moreish and mouthwatering. The skilful blending of spices, seasonings or herbs in varying proportions will enhance the other ingredients and help transform them into all-time favourites.

Starting with flavouring: a good, simple example of this is onion-flavoured vinegar, where the onion is the principal and vinegar the vehicle. Garlic and tomato chutney is another more complex example:

garlic will be the predominant flavour and the
tomato the substance for carrying
that flavour, but in either case, one
will not exist without the other.
Without spices or seasonings,
however, the recipe will be at
best very ordinary, at worst
woefully unpalatable. Strange
combinations can have amazing and agreeable
results, for example lemon, garlic and horseradish;
orange and coriander; rhubarb and vanilla; prunes
and cloves; gooseberry and elderflower; ginger and cardamom. The
real truth of a seasoning is that its presence should not be noticeable
as a single unit, but only as a contribution to the whole, however subtle
or sly the change to the main ingredients.

There are some important points to bear in mind when using spices
in preserve making. Where possible, freshly grind your own spices
as you need them, particularly peppercorns and allspice and freshly
grated nutmeg. It is usually preferable to tie whole spices together in
a muslin bag for all preserves – jams, chutneys, pickles, relishes, etc. –
unless the recipe states otherwise.

When you have to use commercially ground spices, make sure that
they are really fresh, otherwise you will gain nothing from them. So
buy in small quantities and keep in dark, air-tight jars. Throw away
old spices – they are of no use to you. Ground spices are acceptable
in jams and chutneys, but should never be used in clear preserves,
bottling, clear pickles, vinegars or oils, nor added to jellies after they
have been drained through a muslin. The reason for this is quite simple
– the taste will not be impaired, but the result will be as murky as a fish
pond and, in some cases, a thick sediment will form at the bottom of
the jar or bottle, which will look very nasty indeed. You may know that
the product is good, but others will view it with grave suspicion.

Here's a guide to the invaluable spices used in jam, chutney and pickle making:

ALLSPICE

The dried brown berry of *Pimenta dioica*, which grows in tropical America and the West Indies. Similar in appearance to, but smoother than, a peppercorn and tasting of cloves, nutmeg and cinnamon – hence the name. It is also known as Jamaica pepper. This is a particularly useful flavouring for all preserves, pickles and chutneys. Also used in marinades and cakes.

CARDAMOM

True cardamom is either from *Elettaria cardamomum* or *Amomum cardamomum*, which are both members of the ginger family. The tiny black-brown seeds are contained within a creamy green pod and the flavour and smell is distinctly that of eucalyptus – pleasantly aromatic if you like it, but distasteful if you do not. Used mainly in curry powders, it combines well with ginger, coffee and many spices. It is a popular spice in the Middle and Far East, Germany and the Nordic countries. Although not frequently made the most of, cardamom is a very useful spice in pickling, where the taste has been likened to that of a cross between juniper and lime. Most recipes require that you scrape the small seeds from the pods.

CINNAMON

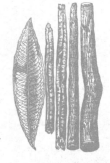

A very valuable spice in preserving. Use either the stick, which is in reality the outer bark of a tree, *Cinnamomum zeylanicum*, which curls into those little scrolls naturally as it dries, or use a ground spice and try to buy a good brand that has not been adulterated with inferior substitutes. Cinnamon is imported mainly from Sri Lanka.

CLOVES

The dried flower buds of *Caryophyllus aromatica*. The name derives from the French for nail, clou, due to the nail-like appearance of the buds. Cloves are tremendously important in preserving, for they are compatible with a vast array of fruit, vegetables, herbs and spices. Prunes, plums, walnuts, apples, oranges, pears and onions can all be pierced with a clove before pickling, spicing or crystallising. Most spice mixtures contain cloves, either ground or whole.

GINGER

An important and endlessly useful spice, ginger is completely universal, being used in everything from flavouring cakes to spicing fish. Coming originally from south China, ginger is the root of *Zingiber officinale*. The fresh root, also known as green ginger, when grated or pounded has a much better flavour than dried root and powdered ginger. Dried ginger goes into all pickling spices and is widely available. Powdered and dried ginger comes from Jamaica and West Africa and neither of them keep their unique taste well. Ginger is used an enormous amount in making preserves and you should always remember that you will only get the best out of your spices if they are fresh. To keep green ginger fresh, put it into a small, clean, dry jar and cover with dry sherry. If the jar is well sealed, this should keep for a long time – the first sign of it deteriorating will be a slight mould.

MACE

The delicate, golden filigree blades of mace are the dried aril or net surrounding the nutmeg, which in turn is the stone of the peach-like fruit *Myristica fragrans*. Blade and ground mace are both expensive, but they provide a distinctive taste which is necessary to many pickles.

NUTMEG

This is the stone or nut of the *Myristica fragrans* fruit. The nut is very hard and can be grated easily to a fine powder using a nutmeg grater. Small graters were once made for this specific purpose, so great was the vogue enjoyed by the nutmeg. It is an essential spice in many sweet pickles, where although it does not predominate, it would certainly be missed if left out. Nutmeg is more versatile than, and can be substituted for, mace. Commercially ground nutmeg can be useful, but it goes stale very quickly and lacks much of the true flavour.

PEPPERCORNS

Black, white, pink and green are all the same berry of *Piper nigrum*, the pepper vine from the Malayan and south Indian forests, Burma and Assam, which produces long, pendulous spikes of small berries, which turn from green to red on ripening. The black peppercorn is the berry picked just as it is beginning to ripen. It is then dried slowly, becoming wrinkled and dark. The outer skin is the aromatic part of the corn. The white peppercorn is the berry when it is allowed to ripen completely and then dried out. An inferior version uses the inside of the black peppercorn after the outer skin has been soaked off, leaving the small, smooth, white centre. Both white and black pepper are best when freshly ground in a peppermill. The black is hot, spicy and aromatic, the white has more of a 'peppery' quality. Green peppercorns are the fresh green berries picked before they are ripe, whilst pink peppercorns are picked when ripe, but not dried, and these are most often packed into jars or tins. Deliciously hot, juicy and soft, pink and green peppercorns, are used most frequently in pâtés and sausages and are really superb in some pickles. No kitchen should be without black and white peppercorns and freshly ground pepper is the premier spice which can be used with flair and imagination in both sweet and savoury dishes. One friend of mine adds several black peppercorns to bottled pears, they discolour a little but certainly add something special. Whole black and white peppercorns are both included in pickling spice.

SAFFRON

The dried pistils of *Crocus sativus* or autumn crocus, which is native to Asia. An integral part of paella, risotto and bouillabaisse, it is the world's most expensive spice. It is rarely used in preserving as the unique, subtle flavour would be wasted, however, when it is called upon to add colour, dried marigold petals are an excellent substitute.

TURMERIC

A bright yellow spice which is mildly pungent, warm and aromatic. An important ingredient in all curry powders and also the most important addition to mustard pickles and piccalillis, it gives no heat but an agreeable spiciness and, of course, the hectic colour. Always buy good-quality turmeric and use it quickly. Like ginger, turmeric is the dried root of a plant – in this case *Curcuma longa*. It is readily available, ground to a fine powder.

VANILLA

The dried seed pod of a Mexican orchid, *Vanilla planifolia*, now grown commercially. Vanilla pods have the appearance of slim, black and sticky-looking pencils, covered in a rime of frost, which is characteristic of the best vanilla pods. Vanilla has many sweet and delicious uses from flavouring milk, ice cream, chocolate and sugar to adding a distinctive flavour to a range of desserts. A vanilla pod can be used time and time again if it is carefully dried and put away in an air-tight jar or stored in a jar of caster sugar so, although it is not cheap, it is an investment. Vanilla's principal uses in preserving are in the syrups for bottled fruits, whole fruit preserves and in jam, although in the latter it is probably more sensible to use a vanilla extract, but do make sure that it is a good one. Don't be mistaken and use vanilla essence – this is a far inferior product and is either a synthetic reproduction or the result of broken pods being soaked in alcohol.

PECTIN

This soluble gum-like carbohydrate is the essential setting agent in jams and jellies. It forms naturally in fruit from pectose during ripening or in fruit and fruit juice by heating. Without pectin, your jam will be a sweet stew and your jelly a syrup. The more pectin that there is in fruit, the more sugar, and sometimes water, you can use, hence more jam. Therefore, it follows that high-pectin fruits like apples are frequently used with those that have a medium or low pectin content in order to make a jam that will set. For example apple and blackberry or apple and strawberry.

Fruits vary in the amount of pectin they contain, so the following is a general guide:

High-pectin fruit: apples, oranges and all citrus fruit, gooseberries, plums, greengages, damsons, quince, all currant fruit, pineapple.
Medium-pectin fruit: pears, apricots, raspberries, blackberries, rhubarb, cherries.
Low-pectin-fruit: strawberries, peaches, nectarines, grapes.

Some fruit, although looking juicy and ripe and coming into the category of high-pectin fruit, will curiously refuse to set. This can be caused by weather conditions – if the fruit has not had much sun, it will not be as high in pectin as expected. Paradoxically, in a very rainy season, plums will swell up deliciously, but will be sadly lacking in flavour and in setting properties. Fruit that is overripe will also lack pectin. These things rarely happen, but if in doubt there is a pectin test you can resort to, although I have to say that it is only worth the hassle if you have a lot of one fruit to use.

TESTING FOR PECTIN

Take a small amount of fruit and proceed as if you were making a jam. Before you reach the sugar stage, take 1 teaspoon of the cooked fruit juice from the pan, cool it in a heatproof glass-lidded jar and add 3 teaspoons methylated spirits. Secure the lid in place and shake the jar. If the result is a nice jelly-like clot, that means that there is a high-pectin content. Small, broken clots mean a medium pectin content and if there are no clots, then there is a poor pectin content and you will have to resort to more devious methods. Do keep the methylated spirit away from utensils, ingredients and naked flames. When making jelly, the pectin content in the fruit juice will be reduced if the juice has been left to drain too long before using and the result will be syrupy.

HOMEMADE PECTIN EXTRACT

This can be obtained from apples (windfalls are the best – there is no point in using expensive, commercially produced apples), redcurrants or gooseberries and it is extremely useful to have as a standby. Measure out your chosen fruit and cold water in the proportions of 1kg fruit to 1 litre water. Wash the fruit making sure that any spoilt pieces are cut away or discarded. Cut the apples into chunks. Put the fruit into a pan with the water, boil together for 30 minutes, pulping and mashing well as you go. Turn into a clean jelly bag and leave to drain right through without prodding. Either use the resulting extract immediately or return it to the clean pan and bring just to the boil. Remove from the heat and pot into small, hot, dry preserving jars. Sterilise for 1–5 minutes (see pages 44–5) – the bigger the jar, the longer the process. I tend to keep my pectin extract in the fridge.

COMMERCIAL PECTIN

Can be used to improve upon, or gain, a set when using medium- or low-pectin fruit. It can also be used to make a more economical jam from all fruit and for making freezer jams. There are specific recipes for these within this book. Pectin additive in crystal form is available in sachets containing 13g pectin each. Use 1 sachet per 800g low-pectin fruit, such as strawberries, and 1kg granulated sugar. The pectin is added with the sugar when the fruit is sufficiently cooked.

CHECKING FOR SETTING POINT

This is a handy check for a set: drop a little boiling jam on to a very cold plate and, after a few seconds, you should be able to tilt the plate without the jam or jelly running. Once you become experienced at making jams, you will recognise the almost magical, glistening translucence of a jam at setting point. The setting point for jelly can be judged by the way in which it will drip very slowly from the spoon. In fact, it almost appears to slowly fold – not run.

OIL

Oil is rarely used in preserving except as an air-tight, flavourless seal for purées and pastes and as a suspension for herbs. In the Middle East, however, delicious locally grown lemons, limes, aubergines and peppers are preserved in oil, whilst from Italy comes a most spectacular pickle called Mostarda di Frutta, which uses mustard seed oil to achieve the unique flavour of this traditional preserve.

In many recipes oil acts as a softening agent instead of salt. The

cheapest and best oils to use in any preserve
are sunflower and rapeseed oil as they are
colourless with no discernible taste. Although
safflower oil is colourless and flavourless,
it is expensive and there would be little
point in using the unusual and expensive
nut and seed oils in recipes where their
gentle flavours might be swamped. Fine
olive oil is rich and fruity, fully redolent of
the Mediterranean regions from which
it comes, but unfortunately its unique
flavour does mask all but the most
robust ingredients, such as garlic
and tomatoes.

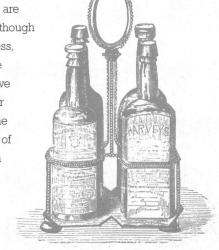

There are plenty of delightful herb
oils – thyme, marjoram, rosemary, etc.
– which have many uses from basting meat and fish to making subtle
and delicate salad dressings. One of the very finest mixed herb oils is
one that I have come across in France and it serves as a good example
for making your own choices, but, do not forget, have fun with your
imagination and make something really different.

To make your own flavoured oil, take a selection of fresh dry herbs
on small branches (pick your own and dry them gently in the oven),
balancing a mixture suitable for a definite purpose, for example thyme,
rosemary, basil, fennel and bay make a pleasant basting oil for meat.
Add a sliver of garlic, several green peppercorns and a little sea salt
for a more aromatic mixture. For a hotter mixture, tiny red chillies can
be added. Arrange these ingredients in an attractive sterilised jar (see
page 44) and fill up with a flavourless fine oil. Seal and leave on a
sunny windowsill for at least 4 weeks before using.

UTENSILS & EQUIPMENT

These may be essential or non-essential, but they are designed to make your life easier and to ensure that cooking becomes a pleasure rather than a chore. They are also designed to prevent mistakes and accidents. Assemble all your equipment before you start otherwise you may find that the jam has burnt whilst you search for that essential wooden spoon.

GENERAL EQUIPMENT

You don't need much specialist equipment for home preserving, but this list covers the basics – many of which you will have already.

GOOD LARGE SCALES OR WEIGHING MACHINE

- Measuring jug with dry and liquid measures and preferably made of rigid polythene or heatproof glass. Also to be used for filling the jars. If you use stainless steel or enamel, you will find that the handles may get very hot.
- A selection of china, heatproof glass or rigid polythene basins or bowls, including several large ones. Do not leave juice to drip into, or fruit or vegetables to stand overnight in, metal basins.
- Several large flat china dishes.
- Wooden spoons: one long handled for stirring volcanic mixtures; one wide and deep for scooping; one flat and short for sieving; one ordinary one for general bashing about.
- Perforated or slotted spoons, ideally wooden. If you use metal, make sure you do not leave it to stand in the pan as it will leave an aftertaste.
- Sharp vegetable knife and a chopping knife.
- Vegetable peeler and corer.
- A potato masher, preferably wooden, for pulping.
- A jelly bag or large squares of clean muslin and a spare piece to cut

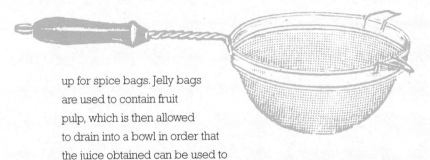

up for spice bags. Jelly bags are used to contain fruit pulp, which is then allowed to drain into a bowl in order that the juice obtained can be used to make a sparklingly clear jelly. Take a square of muslin and lay it, with the edges hanging over, across a colander placed over a deep bowl, throw the fruit pulp and juice into the muslin, gather up the four corners and tie them together, leaving a small loop with which to hang the 'bag' above the bowl. Remove the colander and leave the fruit to drip without pressing. Spice bags are the same thing in miniature and are used to tie whole spices or pips, peelings and cores into. Try not to leave these small bags in the preserve when potting as they can bear an unpleasant resemblance to a dead mouse!

- Large nylon sieve. Do not use metal if you can help it, for it may react against some vegetables and fruit to leave a taste of 'bad pennies'.
- A mallet or blunt instrument for cracking kernels, etc.
- Pestle and mortar or equivalent for pounding and grinding. If you decide to use the end of a wooden rolling pin in a basin, take care not to use too much force – I have knocked the bottom out of more basins than I care to remember.
- Jam funnel and a narrow sauce funnel. Although neither of these is essential, they save waste and prevent the odd accident.
- A juice extractor. To extract pure juice the best piece of equipment is a stand-up metal model with a handle to pull down and squeeze the juice from any citrus fruit without taking peel or pith. It also ensures the maximum amount of juice.
- Measuring spoons.
- Wooden board, clean cloths and oven glove.
- Jam thermometer, which is very handy as it cuts out guesswork.

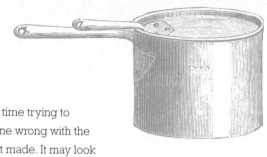

PRESERVING PANS

You can have a very tense time trying to identify what may have gone wrong with the preserve that you have just made. It may look and taste insipid and murky or refuse to set and quite frequently the answer may lie in the pan in which you cooked it.

A few pointers before you start will save you time and trouble:

- A preserving pan should be large enough to take all the ingredients with plenty of room for the contents to rise up without boiling over. The wider the pan, the more quickly the liquid evaporates, hence the more rapid the set.
- Try to use a preserving pan with two-handed grips, not long handles. In this way you will avoid catching the handle whilst working and you will be able to get a far firmer grip on a full, heavy pan. A side-to-side handle across the pan can be dangerous if it catches on its hooks and tips its contents over you and the floor. Remember that unless handles are absolutely well insulated, always wear kitchen gloves when holding pans.
- Heavy-based and preferably copper-clad pans allow a slow and even distribution of heat, which prevents burning when bringing to the boil.
- Do not leave preserves, chutneys, etc. to stand overnight in the preserving pan as this may taint the end product. Pans should be kept scrupulously clean, bright and shiny and if they have been kept in a cupboard, rinse them well before starting.
- Stainless-steel pans are the most satisfactory in every way.
- Enamel pans are passable, but must be free from chips and scratches. However, the contents do tend to burn more easily.

- Cast-iron pans with a good enamel finish and flameproof casseroles may be suitable, but are never very large.
- Copper pans are glorious to look at, but they have several disadvantages. Red fruit will lose its colour when cooked in copper, although green fruit such as gooseberries will stay bright and clear whilst blackcurrants will lose much of their high vitamin C content and also refuse to set. Never cook recipes containing vinegar, for example chutney or pickles, in a copper pan as the vinegar reacts adversely with it and can form a toxic substance. Pickled gherkins, for instance, will look amazingly bright green and professional – they will also be lethal. Fruit and vegetables with high oxalic acid content, such as rhubarb, sorrel and spinach, should not be cooked in copper.
- Aluminium pans. The reasons against using copper pans also apply to aluminium.
- Iron and brass pans should never be used.
- A pressure cooker is both very good for cooking and for sterilising.

ELECTRICAL EQUIPMENT

None of the following are essential, but they will certainly make your life easier:

- A food processor with a slicing and shredding attachment. There are many excellent food processors on the market, but you don't have to go for the top end of the range, you simply need an uncomplicated piece of equipment with variable speeds and an attachment that takes the hard work out of fruit and vegetable preparation.
- A mincer or mincing machine.
- A liquidiser is very handy. Most liquidised pulps have to be sieved as well, but it does cut out the hard labour. A coffee grinder also cuts the hard work out of grinding spices.
- A microwave oven. Follow the manufacturer's instructions for times and quantities as each model varies. The amount of preserve made each time will be limited.

- A slow cooker should be used in the following manner: never fill beyond the manufacturer's advice; make sure that the mixture is hot when it is put into the cooker; and use medium heat. When the fruit, etc. is cooked, turn it out into a pan before adding the sugar and continuing the recipe. Using a slow cooker is useful for softening the peel of citrus fruit and other fruit and vegetables and means that they can be left to cook gently all day without you having to stand over them. A saving in both time and fuel.
- A pressure cooker. This is a useful addition to the home preservers kitchen and instructions for their use can be found under Marmalade (page 175–6).
- A freezer.

JARS, CONTAINERS AND LIDS

Clean, dry, sterilised jars and bottles (see page 44) are suitable for the majority of preserves. Domestic jars, ie jam jars, honey pots, sauce bottles, etc. are accustomed to some heat, but you must make sure that you thoroughly wash and sterilise the jar by heating first. Always use glass bottles with a cork or plastic top to avoid leaving a taint on the finished product, and use a narrow funnel for pouring.

A word about jar sizes. When you come to fill your jam jars you will realise that the British 1lb/450g jar has evolved into a 13oz/375g size. It is difficult to judge exactly how many jars you will need since much depends on the type of fruit or vegetables used and the cooking time. Big, bulky fruit with a high pectin content, like apples, will fill more jars than a shrinking fruit with little pectin content, such as strawberries. Jam containing commercial pectin will give you jam for your money. Chutney and pickles vary considerably depending on the amount of liquid used and the thickness required. It is always wiser to use very small jars or pots (baby food jars are excellent) for more unusual preserves such as herb jellies, which may not be eaten very quickly and may deteriorate once opened. Therefore, you may take it that an ordinary jam jar referred to is the conventional 375g, a medium jar is 175g and a small jar is approximately 50–75g. Large jars, generally speaking, hold 900g.

Jars can be sealed with wax discs and paper or small rounds of pretty material or paper doilies tied down with string, which is a very attractive option for giving as presents. Screw-top lids can be used to seal any preserve that does not contain vinegar as vinegar corrodes metal and not only makes a nasty mess, but renders the contents unobtainable. However, many jar and bottle caps are now plastic lined.

Strictly speaking, corks should not be used in herb vinegars as they tend to draw out flavour, although many corks are now made from plastic. If in doubt, make a tight twist of greaseproof paper around the bottom of the cork. Bottle corks may be obtained from ironmongers. Make sure that they are clean and dry before using.

When potting with Kilner or preserving jars, always use new bands and the lids and screw or clip seals provided with the jars. An old-fashioned and very competent way of sealing preserves is to pour a thin layer of paraffin wax over the contents, but this has its disadvantages: the preserve must be really thick and well set and besides, it is a very fiddly business.

Some of the recipes for pickles refer to the use of earthenware jars. Although earthenware jars are the traditional containers for pickled fruits and fruits in alcohol, certain facts must be established. First, do make sure that the container is fully glazed and non-porous, otherwise your lovely juice will disappear. Secondly, if it is glazed, it must not be a lead glaze. Lead reacts against vinegar, alcohol and certain fruit with a high acid content to become potentially lethal. Those attractive old-fashioned earthenware containers picked up at car-boot sales and second-hand shops may be lead glazed for in Britain and on the Continent this was predominantly used in the past. Scandinavian countries favoured a borax or salt glaze and these are the ones most frequently used nowadays. A rough guide is in the appearance: borax and salt glazes are usually of a speckled grey stone. Nowadays those highly decorative rumtopf and pickle jars, which have been made specifically for those purposes, one would assume to be safe, but if you are not sure, do not use them.

Clean and polish your containers after you have filled them, label them clearly with the contents and date and store them in a cool dry place away from bright lights, damp, steam and well off concrete floors. Now you can sit back, quite smugly, and enjoy the sight of rows of glowing, glistening and glorious preserves, which are the fruits of your imagination, hard work and labour.

TO STERILISE GLASS BOTTLES OR JARS BEFORE FILLING

Preheat the oven to 120°C/gas mark ½. Wash the bottles or jars and lids in very hot soapy water, rinse and then place in a roasting tray. Pour boiling water into the jars and bottles and over the lids. Discard the water and then place the tray in the preheated oven for 15 minutes. The bottles or jars and lids are then ready to use.

If you put a cold glass jar straight into a hot oven or boiling water it will crack. The same applies to transferring hot jars full of hot preserve on to a cold surface, so lay a wooden board or thick cloth where you intend to place the jars. Decorative glass jars are a different thing and should be carefully tested for their strength before filling with a hot preserve.

TO STERILISE FILLED JARS

This process is used for the final stages of all the sauce, purée and paste recipes. The jars to use for preserves that need sterilising after potting are the four-piece preserving jars with rubber bands, glass lids, screw or clip tops. Before you start cooking your fruit take your clean, dry jars and pop them into a cool oven and bring the heat up to 140°C/gas mark 1. Put the tops of the jars to boil for 10 minutes, bringing the heat up from cold. Just before they are done, drop the rubber bands in as well.

Pour the boiling preserve into the jars. Put on the rubber bands and the tops. Fasten the tops of the jars with screw lids or clips. When using screw lids, give a bare half turn back again to allow for the expansion of the jars. Put a wire rack or false bottom in a preserving pan. Stand the jars in the receptacle, making sure that they do not touch and fill the container with very hot water. Bring to the boil and boil for 5–8 minutes or however long is specified in the recipe. Remove the jars and place on a wooden board or thick cloth. Tighten the screw tops immediately.

Test after 24 hours by removing the clip or screw band – you should be able to lift the jar by the glass tops. If the jar does not fall off, then the seal is complete. If it does fall off, then you will either have to scrape the contents from the floor or eat it within the next few days. This principal is the same as that for bottling fruit and vegetables. Asparagus pans, tall and narrow, are excellent for sterilising bottles.

STORING PRESERVES

As the reason for making preserves is in order to put produce by for another day, it would be expected that jams, preserves, chutneys, sauces and pickles, etc. should last for at least 6 months if they have been made and potted correctly, and most probably longer. Use within a year to be absolutely certain.

Most preserves, unless specifically stated otherwise, can be eaten as soon as they are cooled – usually the next day.

Some preserves, like lemon curd which has eggs and butter in it, are better kept in the fridge once opened.

Chutney will shrink quite considerably over time as it thickens on keeping, so make sure the jar is well filled.

WHAT WENT WRONG?

Nothing can make the keen home preserver weep more copiously than the discovery that all of those glorious well-made pots have 'gone off'. The waste of time, effort and money is very defeating, but all is not lost. The least problematic is a little growth of fluffy mould on the top of sweet preserves and I am assured that providing the product is homemade, does not smell 'winey' or fermenting and has no other discernible bad smell or look, this can be removed. Clean the lid and dry, then replace, keep in the fridge and consume the preserve quickly. I speak from experience.

However, it is so much better to avoid these problems from the start. Apart from problems such as the incorrect use of sugar, fermenting caused by overripe or bruised fruit, or poor colour due to the wrong pan being used, the most common problem of storing jam is that of a mould forming on top.

The most likely cause is an oversight during the potting process. Jars must be scrupulously dried, sterilised (see page 44) and, unless stated otherwise, hot. The jar should be filled carefully to ensure that no air bubbles are trapped (the best way of achieving this is to give the jar one or two taps – doesn't always work, but often does) and the preserve should reach almost to the top. Jam and jellies shrink on cooling and, not only does this look a bit off, it also means that the chances of a mould forming are greater. As said earlier, chutney and robust pickles will also shrink and thicken on keeping and unless the pot is fully filled, the contents will end up halfway down the jar.

Another cause that I have found is sealing the jar when the preserve is warm. Do one of two things as the recipe states: either seal it as soon as it is potted, providing the jam, etc. is boiling or, if you have waited for it to cool (in the case of whole fruit preserves) to give a better dispersal of fruit, then allow it to become quite cold before sealing. The jar should be properly sealed with wax discs and a lid or cellophane tied down with a rubber band. Cellophane covers should be checked from time to time during keeping to make sure that they have not perished. Store all preserves in cool, dry cupboards away from bright lights, damp, steam and well off concrete floors.

SAFETY IN THE KITCHEN

Boiling jam, syrup or chutney can cause some of the worse scalds and burns imaginable, so never, ever leave your children alone in the kitchen when you are preserving or, better still, do not let them in at all when they are small. If they have to be in the kitchen, make sure that all pans are on the back plates and no handles are sticking out.

For your own protection, never wear flowing sleeves or unbuttoned cardigans, which may catch on, or trail in, the pan. They may also catch on unexpected protuberances in the kitchen and jar the arm that is holding a pan full of boiling contents.

Try to use preserving pans with two-handed grips, not long handles. In this way, you avoid catching the handle as you move around and it also gives you a firm two-handed grip on the pan. All old-fashioned preserving pans were made in this way. A side-to-side handle across the pan can also be dangerous if it catches on its hooks and tips the contents on to your floor, front or feet. Unless handles are absolutely insulated, wear kitchen gloves for holding them.

Always use the back rings of the cooker and keep the pan away from the front where it can tip over and where you have to lean across it. Long-handled wooden spoons are invaluable, for wood does not conduct heat and the long handle will protect you against popping bubbles of erupting jam, etc. Wear an oven glove to protect your hand. A solid plastic measuring jug and funnel make filling jars much easier and, if you stand the jars on a thick cloth or wooden board, this will prevent them from slipping or cracking. Wipe up any liquid or pieces of fruit or vegetable skin, etc, that may have dropped on the floor and try to think of wearing flat-soled, well-fitting shoes.

VEGET

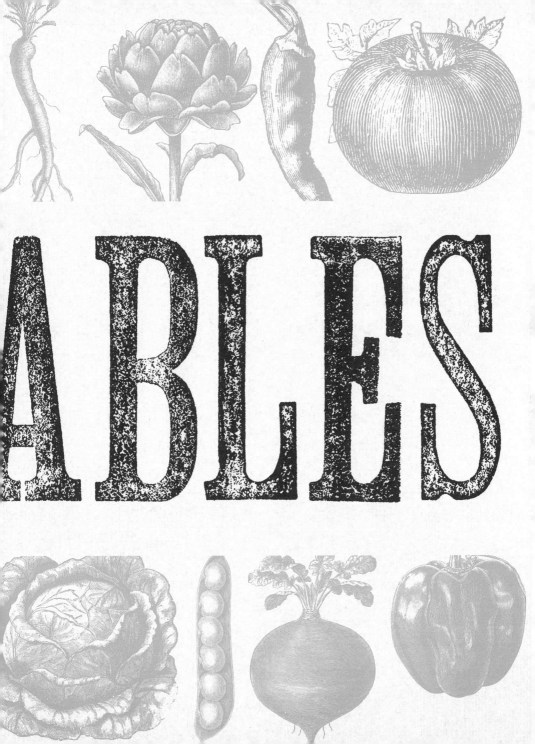

ARTICHOKE

There are two different types of artichokes readily available in the UK. The globe artichoke is the blue-green thistly plant, which throws out spectacular blue flowers if left too long (by which time the coveted heart will be of no use, so cut off the heads before they open out). Most globe artichokes are imported.

The Jerusalem artichoke is a very decorative plant, but the root is the part that is used as a vegetable. Knobbly and difficult to peel, it has the most unique, rather smoky, nutty taste, which many people find very appealing.

Artichoke Pickle

I think this pickle goes superbly well with smoked fish. The lemon gives a strange pungency to the delicate nutty flavour of the artichoke and it also has the added advantage of looking attractive and unusual. Don't throw the vinegar away – it is excellent in its own right and particularly good with fish or in a salad dressing or mayonnaise.

MAKES 3 X 375G JARS

1kg Jerusalem artichokes

50g sea salt

2 lemons

4 bay leaves

1.5 litres white malt vinegar

3 x 375g sterilised jam jars (page 44)

Wash the artichokes and scrub them well with a small brush. Peel them (this is a tricky business, but it's got to be done properly). Cut any large artichokes in half and drop them all into a pan of boiling water to which you have added the 50g salt. Cover and cook until just tender; do not overcook because they are liable to disintegrate.

Whilst they are cooking, take the peel from the lemons in thin strips with a vegetable peeler, removing the pith as you go. Put this with the bay leaves and vinegar into a pan and boil for 15 minutes. Allow the vinegar to cool, drain off and keep the peel and bay leaves.

When the artichokes are just cooked, drain them and pack them carefully into the jars, dispersing the peel and bay leaves decoratively amongst them. Pour the cold vinegar over the contents of the jars to cover completely. Seal and label.

Keep for at least 4 weeks before using.

Globe Artichoke Pickle

This is an amazing pickle. If fresh artichokes are unavailable or you are a bit pushed for time, with discretion, tinned artichoke hearts can be used here instead.

MAKES 3 X 500ML JARS

12 small globe artichoke hearts or bottoms
1 tablespoon lemon juice
600ml white wine or white malt vinegar
24 small white pearl onions
50g black raisins
3 pinches of white granulated sugar
3 pinches of sea salt
3 thin strips of lemon rind
3 small garlic cloves, peeled
3 fresh basil leaves
1 litre white wine or cider vinegar
3 bay leaves
3 x 500ml wide-necked sterilised jam jars
(preferably Kilner jars) (page 44)

Place the artichokes in a large pan, cover them with cold water and add the lemon juice, bring to the boil and simmer for 7 minutes. Drain and place in a large china bowl. Remove the outer foliage until the heart appears. Cut it out, remove the choke, trim and return the hearts to the bowl, cover with the white vinegar and leave overnight.

The next day, peel the onions and blanch them briefly in boiling water. Rinse the raisins in boiling water. Drain the artichoke hearts.

Into each jar place a pinch of sugar and a pinch of salt, 1 piece of lemon peel, 1 peeled garlic clove and 1 basil leaf. Pack the jars with an equal amount of artichoke hearts, onions and raisins and place them on a thick cloth.

Bring the white wine or white malt vinegar briefly to the boil and pour slowly over the contents of the jars (although commercial jam jars are pretty heatproof it is wiser to pour the hot liquid into them slowly and to keep the work surface protected). Add a bay leaf to each jar, seal tightly and label.

Keep for at least 1 week before using and tip each jar gently every day to allow the flavours to circulate.

BEAN

What a beautifully evocative word bean is, summing up the best in British vegetables. Everybody, no matter how small the space allotted them, should be able to grow at least one variety and reap a modest crop, for beans are accommodating, good-natured and productive.

The one bean that I would grow above all others is the broad bean. The white scented flowers with long, soft, green pods velvet-coated inside, provide soft hollows for the large, flat, green or white bean. When young, the beans are excellent lightly blanched and eaten in salads and they are also very good pickled.

French beans, dwarf or stringless beans are smooth and rounded, requiring only topping and tailing. Runner or scarlet beans are longer and flatter than French beans and have to be strung and sliced before cooking. Both of these green beans are abundant croppers and British-grown ones should be widely available. Recipes including French and runner beans are dotted throughout this book as they make more interesting pickles when used in conjunction with other vegetables and fruit.

Pickled Broad Beans

Pickled broad beans are a wonderful addition to the hors d'oeuvre table and make a stunning present – especially if given with a jar of Pickled Artichokes (page 51).

MAKES 2 X 375G JARS

1kg unpodded broad beans

2 teaspoons sea salt

1 orange

1 garlic clove

2 cardamom pods

2.5cm piece of dried root ginger

1 teaspoon cumin seeds

600ml white malt vinegar

2 x 375g sterilised jam jars (page 44)

Shell the beans and do not be alarmed at the meagre remains of your kilogram. Put them in a pan of boiling water to which you have added the salt. Boil gently until they are just soft, but if the beans break up they will ruin the pickle, so bite one and see. The skin should be firm, but the inside soft. Strain the beans and leave them to cool.

Pare a few strips of rind from the orange, peel and crush the garlic, scrape the seeds from the cardamom pods, bruise the ginger and put all of these and the cumin seeds into the pan with the vinegar. Boil for 10 minutes and then remove from the heat.

Allow the vinegar to become quite cold before straining it (reserve the orange rind). Pack the beans carefully into the jars, taking great care that they do not break or mash. Place a few pieces of orange rind amongst them for decorative effect. Pour the cold vinegar over them to cover completely, making sure there are no air bubbles. Seal and label.

Keep for at least 2 weeks before using.

Mixed Summer Pickle

This is a useful recipe with which you can experiment using a variety of different vegetables. Without the chilli it is mild and unassuming, with the chilli it is quite fiery.

MAKES 3 X 375G JARS

450g runner beans
450g small shallots or pickling onions
225g cauliflower
225g cucumber
1 red pepper
1 fresh red chilli (optional)
several bay leaves
100g sea salt
175g white granulated sugar
900ml white malt vinegar
3 x 375g sterilised jam jars (page 44)

Wash and string the beans and cut them into smallish chunks. Peel the onions. Remove the leaves and stalk from the cauliflower and separate into small, neat florets. Wash the cucumber and cut in half, scoop out the seeds, and cut into large dice. Cut the pepper into strips, discarding the seeds, and shred the chilli, taking great care to keep the volatile oils away from your eyes.

Place all the prepared ingredients into a large bowl with the bay leaves, sprinkle with the salt and mix well. Cover and leave to stand in a cool place for 24 hours.

Drain the vegetables and rinse them well under cold running water, drain and pat dry with a clean tea towel. Remove the bay leaves. Pack the vegetables into the jars, leaving a 2.5cm space at the top.

Dissolve the sugar in 225ml of the vinegar over a low heat, cool and add the remaining vinegar. Pop a bay leaf into each jar and pour the vinegar over to cover completely. Tip and tilt a little to remove any air bubbles. Seal tightly and label.

Keep for at least 1 week before using.

BEETROOT

Beetroot is an ancient vegetable, which was very popular with the Romans. When cooked it is sweet and tasty. It is most familiar when pickled, but it also makes an excellent hot vegetable and a traditional soup. Beetroots may be steamed, boiled or baked in the oven in a tightly lidded dish with a small amount of water. Do not boil beetroot too hard or for too long – a large, fresh beet will take about two hours to boil. Try not to cut the green tops or the root off the beetroot or to damage or score the skin prior to cooking or the beet will bleed and lose its colour. After cooking and while the beetroot is still hot, rub your finger and thumb over the skin, which will come away in your hand, taking the tops and tails with it.

Apart from the familiar ruby red beetroot, there is now a golden beetroot and a white one. And, as a bonus, it's worth remembering all young beetroot have deliciously edible leaves.

Sweet Beetroot Pickle

This makes a nice change from the ubiquitous pickled beetroot in vinegar – the spices add a kick and the sugar brings out the sweet beetroot flavour.

MAKES 3 X 375G JARS

1.1 litres malt vinegar

3cm piece of cinnamon stick

6 cloves

2 blades mace

7 whole allspice

1 small dried chilli

500g soft brown sugar

1kg beetroot

3 x 375g sterilised jam jars (page 44)

Place the vinegar in a pan with the spices, bring to the boil and boil hard for 2 minutes. Cover and leave to get cold.

Strain and bring to the boil again, then add the sugar, stirring well to make sure it is dissolved, and cook gently until the mixture turns slightly syrupy. Set aside to cool.

Wash, prepare and cook the beetroot in boiling, salted water until tender. Whilst still warm, remove their skins. Leave to get cold then slice or dice them.

Pack the jars with the beetroot and cover with the syrupy vinegar.

Seal and label.

Keep for at least 2 weeks before using.

Beetroot Chutney

A nice earthy chutney, which complements cheeses.

MAKES 4 X 375G JARS

1kg beetroot

350g onions

1 garlic clove

450ml white malt vinegar

350g hard cooking, eating or windfall apples

250g sultanas

1 teaspoon pickling spice

2.5cm piece of dried root ginger

1 tablespoon finely grated lemon zest

1 dessertspoon grated horseradish

350g white granulated sugar

small muslin bag for spices

4 x 375g sterilised jam jars (page 44)

Wash, prepare and cook the beetroot in boiling, salted water until tender. When cool, peel and dice them.

Peel and chop the onions and garlic, put them into a large pan with a little of the vinegar and cook until soft. Wash, peel, core and dice the apples. Wash the sultanas, tie the pickling spices in the muslin bag, bruise the ginger, and put these, with the apples, beetroot, lemon zest, horseradish and half the remaining vinegar, into the pan with the onion and garlic. Cook until very soft, stirring occasionally and taking care not to burn.

Add the remaining vinegar and the sugar to the pan, heat gently, stirring well until the sugar has dissolved. Boil steadily until the chutney is thick. Remove the spice bag. Carefully pour into the jars and seal and label.

Keep for at least 1 month before using.

CABBAGE

There are so many varieties of cabbage, but the one cabbage preferred by the enthusiastic home preserver is definitely the red cabbage – a very firm round cabbage, which is just marvellous when pickled. When preparing cabbage, it is necessary to remove the thick white ribs and stalks before slicing it. I use the shredder attachment on my mixer for this as, when pickling, I find it gives a finer and less erratic result than hand slicing and it is so much easier.

And once you've finished your jar of pickled red cabbage, don't just discard the remaining vinegar – heated up and drunk it is an antidote (albeit a rather strong one...) to tickly coughs.

Hot and Spicy Pickled Red Cabbage

A fiery pickled cabbage, which gives rise to a sharp intake of breath. If you would prefer a milder vinegar, halve the amount of each spice and leave out the chillies and garlic.

MAKES 4 X 375G JARS

1kg firm red cabbage

sea salt, for sprinkling

1.2 litres malt vinegar

15g black peppercorns

8 blades mace

6 bay leaves

2 x 4cm pieces of dried root ginger, bruised

5cm piece of cinnamon stick

4 dried chillies, crushed

1 tablespoon cloves

1 tablespoon mustard seeds

1 tablespoon whole allspice

1 teaspoon sea salt

1 garlic clove, crushed

4 x 375g sterilised jam jars (page 44)

Wash the outside of the cabbage and throw away any discoloured leaves. Halve and quarter it and remove the white stalk and ribs. Cut into strips across the cabbage – this way you get nice fine shreds, not great floppy hunks. I do this on a shredder and it does make shorter shreds, which you may prefer. Lay the cabbage in a large dish or basin and sprinkle each layer with sea salt. Cover and leave for 24 hours.

Meanwhile, make the spicy vinegar by boiling all the remaining ingredients together for 5 minutes. Cover and leave to cool. Then strain and set aside until ready to use.

The next day, tip the cabbage into a colander to drain off any surplus salt, rinse under cold running water if necessary, and drain again. Pat dry and then pack the cabbage loosely into the jars and pour the spicy vinegar over to cover. Leave a short while for the vinegar to permeate and any air bubbles to rise, then press down to see if it needs topping up with more vinegar. Seal and label.

Keep for 2 weeks before using, but use within 3 months or it will go soft.

Red Cabbage Relish

A softer cabbage preserve than the spicy pickled cabbage, this is ideal for spreading and is particularly good in cold meat sandwiches.

MAKES 3 X 375G JARS

1kg firm red cabbage

sea salt, for sprinkling

2.5cm piece of dried root ginger, bruised

1 teaspoon caraway seeds

1 teaspoon whole allspice

4 blades mace

15g white granulated sugar

finely grated zest of ½ orange

1.2 litres white malt vinegar

small muslin bag for spices

3 x 375g sterilised jam jars (page 44)

Wash the outer cabbage leaves, removing any blemished pieces. Halve and quarter the cabbage, cutting out the white stalk and ribs. Grate on a coarse grater or use a shredder attachment. Place the cabbage in a deep bowl, sprinkling each layer with salt as you go. Cover and leave for 24 hours.

The next day, drain the cabbage in a colander and rinse it briefly under cold running water. Shake well to remove any excess moisture and leave to drain.

Meanwhile, place the spices in the muslin bag and put this with the sugar, orange zest and vinegar into a pan. Bring to the boil, stirring to dissolve the sugar, and boil for 3 minutes, then reduce to barely simmering. Cover and leave for 10 minutes.

Return the drained cabbage to the bowl, remove the muslin bag from the vinegar and pour the hot vinegar over the cabbage. Cover and leave for 24 hours, giving it an occasional stir.

Pack the cabbage into the jars, making sure it is well covered with vinegar. If it isn't, heat up a little more vinegar and use this to top up. Seal.

Keep for at least 1 week before using.

CELERY

As I have consigned more than one crop of celery to the compost heap, I do not consider my advice on the subject of growing it to be of any value! Nor do I consider the pale and anaemic polythene-wrapped variety to be worth buying, finding that dirty celery (from a market, farm shop or, if you have more luck than me, your own garden!) when well washed, to be infinitely preferable. The good, firm, white sticks tinged with green are crisp and well-flavoured and make super pickles and an excellent vinegar, which can be used in salad dressings and mayonnaise.

Celery and Tomato Relish

A gentle, flavoursome relish.

MAKES 6 X 375G JARS

2 heads of celery

500g tomatoes

1 red pepper

1 green pepper

8 medium-sized onions

2 large garlic cloves

300ml white malt vinegar

150g white granulated sugar

2 teaspoons sea salt

½ teaspoon mustard powder

½ teaspoon ground allspice

½ teaspoon ground cinnamon

½ teaspoon celery seeds

6 x 375g sterilised jam jars (page 44)

Wash the celery thoroughly, taking care to remove all the mud. Remove the leaves and chop the stalks into 12mm pieces. Drop the tomatoes into boiling water, then into cold. Skin and chop them. Wash and chop the peppers, removing the seeds and pith. Peel and chop the onions and garlic.

Put the vinegar into a pan with the sugar, salt and spices, bring gently to the boil, stirring well until all is dissolved, and boil together for 5 minutes. Add the vegetables, bring to the boil again and then simmer gently for about 40 minutes, giving an occasional stir. Pot, seal and label.

Keep for at least 1 week before using.

Celery Vinegar

Many vegetables such as celeriac and fennel can be used to flavour vinegar by this method and it is wonderful in mayonnaise, salad dressings and sauces.

MAKES 3 X 500ML BOTTLES

1 head of celery

1.5 litres white malt vinegar

1 tablespoon sea salt

1 tablespoon white granulated sugar

3 x 500g sterilised jam jars

muslin cloth for straining

3 x 500ml sterilised bottles (page 44)

Wash and scrub the celery thoroughly and cut it into small pieces.

Put the vinegar, salt and sugar into a pan and bring to the boil. Remove from the heat. Pack the celery into the jars and cover completely with the vinegar. Seal tightly and leave for 2 weeks to macerate.

Strain through a muslin cloth. Bottle, seal and label.

You can start using the finished vinegar straight away. Although it keeps well, the flavour will deteriorate after 6 months, so do use it up quickly.

CHILLI

There are many different varieties of chillies with varying degrees of heat, of which the best-known hot one is the Scotch Bonnet. It usually appears that the smaller they are, the hotter they are. Dorset seems to have taken over as the chilli centre of England since two enterprising young men set up a chilli farm in the Dorset countryside. Having gained a reputation for growing some of the hottest chillies ever, the farm has gone from strength to strength and the chillies it produces are used in everything from relishes to chocolates and ice cream.

Every country I have ever been to has had some other variation of the name and this lack of ethnic knowledge has led to some very nasty assaults on my taste buds! Nevertheless, I still consider chilli an indispensable ingredient – but only in careful quantities. When cutting chillies, take care not to touch the lips, eyes or other sensitive areas with your fingers as the residual oils cause a painful burning sensation. Douse any affected area with cold water or just grin and bear it…!

Chilli Relish

A hot relish, wonderful for barbecues, which can be made hotter or milder by the amount of chillies used.

MAKES 8 X 175G JARS

10 whole fresh chillies or 6 whole dried chillies

450g onions

2 fat garlic cloves

450g ripe tomatoes

450g cooking apples

225g sultanas

1 dessertspoon mustard seeds

1 dessertspoon whole allspice

1 dessertspoon cloves

1 dessertspoon sea salt

600ml white or brown malt vinegar

225g soft light brown sugar

2 small muslin bags for chillies and spices

8 x 175g sterilised jam jars (page 44)

Wash and shred the fresh chillies. Tie the prepared fresh or dried chillies in a muslin bag. Peel and chop the onions and garlic. Wash and chop the tomatoes. Peel, core and chop the apples.

Bruise the spices and tie them into the second muslin bag. Put all the remaining ingredients into a large pan, stirring well to dissolve the sugar and bring gently to the boil. Reduce the heat and simmer gently until the mixture is very thick, taking care not to let it stick or burn.

When it is nicely thick and soft, remove both muslin bags and put the mixture into a blender and briefly whizz it – you can use a mincer, which is very messy but does give a chunkier sauce. Return to the pan and reheat to boiling, giving an occasional stir. Pot, seal and label.

Keep for at least 1 week before using. This relish keeps for at least 6 months and is best kept in the fridge once opened.

Pickled Mixed Chilli Peppers

A Mexican-inspired pickle, which is elegant, attractive and very useful in the kitchen as an ingredient or garnish. The chillies are also a stupendous addition to the hors d'oeuvre tray, but do warn your guests!

MAKES 1 X 375G JAR

225g fresh chillies

600ml white wine or cider vinegar

2 teaspoons white granulated sugar

3 garlic cloves

1 small dried red chilli

1 teaspoon coriander seeds

1 teaspoon cloves

2 bay leaves

1 x 375g wide-necked sterilised jar (page 44)

Simmer the chillies in water for 5 minutes. Remove with caution and lay out on a clean tea towel to drain and dry.

Warm the vinegar, add the sugar and bring briefly to the boil. Remove from the heat and leave to cool. Peel and crush the garlic. Crush the dried chilli, coriander seeds and cloves. Place half of these in the bottom of the jar with one bay leaf. Pack in the chillies, add the remaining garlic, spices and bay leaf. Pour over the vinegar to cover. Seal tightly and label.

Leave for at least 1 month to mature. And if you like it really hot...

Another simple and effective tear jerker is to pack a sterilised jam jar with chillies that you have pierced with a needle and cover them with dry sherry. Seal tightly, label and leave for at least 1 month. They can be used in the same way as the pickled mixed chilli peppers, and the sherry makes a terrific addition to dressings and sauces.

CUCUMBER

Cucumbers are not the greatest vegetable to preserve, but they do frequently appear in glut proportions so it is handy to have some ideas for use beyond that of the salad bowl. Cucumbers are usually left for a short period of time in some kind of salt preparation prior to pickling, and it is worth remembering that a dry brine gives a crisper end result than a wet brine. Most of these recipes are a simple extension of making use of a glut vegetable, which is usually the standard greenhouse variety that faithfully reappears throughout the year. Very rarely you may come across ridge or pickling cucumbers or gherkins

and it is worth looking in local produce markets for them as they make superior pickles.

Marsha's Cucumber Relish

This recipe came from my American friend, Marsha, and it's a simple relish with a good flavour. Light mild pickles, such as this one, are called bread and butter pickles in the States because they can be spread on bread for a tasty snack.

MAKES 4 X 375G JARS

6 good-sized, firm cucumbers
½ head celery
1 red pepper
1 green pepper
500g onions
50g sea salt
425ml cider vinegar
300g white granulated sugar
1 level tablespoon mustard seeds
1 dessertspoon celery seeds
1 teaspoon turmeric
4 x 375g sterilised jam jars (page 44)

Peel and cut the cucumbers in half, lengthways, and remove the seeds (best done with a spoon). Cut the cucumber into small chunky dice. Wash the celery well and chop into small pieces. Wash, deseed and cut the peppers into small chunks. Peel, slice and finely chop the onions. If you want finely chopped veg, pop several small batches into a food processor at a time, but remember that the cucumber may disintegrate.

Put the vegetables into a large bowl, sprinkling with the salt as you go, and turn the mixture over with your hands. Cover and leave overnight.

The next day, throw the vegetables into a colander to drain for 2 hours, again using your hands to turn the vegetables and shaking from time to time to help release the salty juices.

Put the mixture into a pan with the remaining ingredients, bring gently to the boil and boil for approximately 15 minutes or until the pickle is well cooked, but still with a crunchy texture. Pot, seal and label.

Keep for at least 2 weeks before using.

Easy Mustard Pickle

There is no doubt that you either love or loathe mustard pickle. Without the chillies, this is a mild and respectable pickle, with them, it is somewhat fiery.

MAKES 5 X 375G JARS

500g cucumbers

500g courgettes or marrows

250g green beans

250g pickling onions or shallots

200g sea salt

900ml malt vinegar

175g soft light brown sugar

6 whole fresh red chillies or 3 dried chillies (optional)

1 tablespoon plain flour

3 teaspoons mustard powder

3 teaspoons turmeric

5 x 375g sterilised jam jars (page 44)

Peel, deseed and dice the cucumbers and courgettes or marrows. String and slice the beans crosswise. Peel the onions and leave whole if they are very small, otherwise cut in half. Put all the vegetables into a large china bowl. Dissolve the salt in 2 litres cold water and cover the vegetables with this brine. Place a plate on top of the mixture to keep it submerged, and leave for 24 hours.

Drain, rinse well and pat dry on tea towels. Pour the vinegar, less 2 tablespoons, into a large pan with the sugar and shred the chillies, if using, and add them to the pan. Bring to the boil, stirring constantly, until the sugar is dissolved. Boil for 3 minutes, then add the vegetables. Simmer for a further 5 minutes.

In the meantime, mix the flour, mustard powder and turmeric to a smooth paste with the remaining 2 tablespoons vinegar. Add this to the vegetables, stirring continuously until boiling. Simmer for a further 10 minutes, stirring occasionally. Pot, seal and label.

Keep for at least 2 weeks before using.

Cucumber and Tomato Pickle

This is a sweet, delicious pickle, which is popular with everyone from the youngest to the oldest.

MAKES 5 X 375G JARS

500g cucumbers

2 teaspoons sea salt

250g onions

500g ripe tomatoes

1 green pepper

1 red pepper

175g sultanas

bunch of fresh mint

600ml cider vinegar

1 teaspoon curry powder

1 teaspoon mustard powder

½ teaspoon cayenne pepper

½ teaspoon paprika

½ teaspoon ground ginger

½ teaspoon ground black pepper

250g white granulated or soft brown sugar

5 x 375g sterilised jam jars (page 44)

Peel, deseed and dice the cucumbers. Place in a bowl and sprinkle with the salt. Peel and finely chop the onions. Plunge the tomatoes into boiling water, then into cold, and the skins should come off as if by magic; chop the pulp. Wash the peppers and dice them, removing the pith and seeds. Wash and chop the sultanas. Wash and finely chop the mint (or put it into a liquidiser with a little of the vinegar and, hey presto!).

Put the vinegar and spices into a large pan and bring to the boil. Drain and remove any excess salt from the cucumbers and add these to the pan with the other vegetables, sultanas, mint and sugar. Heat gently, stirring well, until the sugar has dissolved. Bring to the boil and simmer for about 1 hour, depending on how lush the tomatoes are, until well cooked and thick. Pot, seal and label.

Keep for at least 1 week before using.

GARLIC

Garlic is one of the most universally loved, hated, abused, overworked or neglected seasonings in creation. Whether you love it or loathe it, garlic is absolutely essential to many dishes and such should be the expertise of the cook, it should never be overwhelming. Garlic is used extensively in both fruit and vegetable pickles and chutneys, where its underlying pungency gives depth to the preserve, bringing out the best in other ingredients. Some of the best British garlic is grown on the Isle of Wight, where they have an annual festival to celebrate the harvest – I am always stunned by the many varieties on offer.

Persian Pickled Garlic

This is a very traditional recipe from old Persia, where a jar of pickled garlic would be left for many years before eating, by which time it becomes thick and jammy with no discernible pungency. So for a truly authentic touch, you should really bury the pot in the garden for a year or two! The best garlic to use are those great fat bulbs that you can buy on a rope.

MAKES 1 X 1 LITRE KILNER JAR

500g garlic cloves

1 tablespoon coriander seeds

12 black peppercorns

2 dried red chillies

1 tablespoon sea salt

a few sprigs of dried thyme

1 litre robust cider or red wine vinegar

1 x 1 litre sterilised Kilner jar (page 44)

Peel the garlic cloves. Slightly crush the coriander and peppercorns and shred the chillies. Mix the spices and salt together. Place a layer of garlic in the jar, followed by a sprinkling of spices and a sprig of thyme. Continue layering in this manner until all the ingredients are used up, and then completely cover them with the vinegar. Seal tightly and label.

Shake the jar gently every day for 1 week. Then leave for at least 1 month before using.

Worcester Sauce

Another roof-raiser that is probably best labelled 'high explosive'. This pungent sauce is very versatile and can add a boost to stews, sauces and casseroles, marinades and dressings. The homemade version is more savoury and, whilst very hot, not as searing as the commercial variety.

MAKES 2 X 500ML BOTTLES

6 large garlic cloves

50g shallots

600ml malt vinegar

2 teaspoons grated fresh horseradish

2 teaspoons cayenne pepper

6 whole cloves

4 x 6cm pieces of dried root ginger, bruised

seeds from 1 cardamom pod

10 black peppercorns

4 tablespoons soy sauce

2 teaspoons soft brown sugar

1 x 1 litre sterilised Kilner jar (page 44)

muslin cloth for straining

narrow funnel

2 x 500ml sterilised glass bottles (page 44)

Peel and chop the garlic and shallots, put them in a pan with the vinegar and bring to the boil. Simmer gently for 15 minutes, add the remaining ingredients and simmer for a further 30 minutes.

Pour into the Kilner jar and cover securely. Leave to macerate for 1 month, shaking well each day.

Strain through a muslin cloth and decant into two bottles, using a narrow funnel. Seal tightly and label.

This will keep almost indefinitely, becoming stronger with age.

HORSERADISH

Many people have strong feelings about horseradish, they either shudder at the thought or love it. Once a plant is established in a quiet spot in the garden, it will flourish and go on forever. Its abundant, bright green foliage make it a great backdrop for other plants, but if you are going to use it, leave plenty of space to dig in and chop a chunk off the root.

The root is pungently hot and peppery and the fumes from fresh, raw horseradish will make your eyes water, therefore it is advisable, when you have washed and scraped it, to leave it to stand for an hour or so in a bowl of cold water.

Basic Horseradish Sauce

A basic traditional horseradish sauce is usually made by mixing grated horseradish with cream to serve with roast beef, but try mixing it with apple or gooseberry purée to make an unusual accompaniment to mackerel or sausages.

MAKES 4 X 175G JARS

1 large piece of fresh horseradish (approx. 800g before peeling)

4 teaspoons sea salt

2 teaspoons white granulated sugar

a few dried red chillies (optional)

white malt vinegar

double cream, apple or gooseberry purée, to serve

4 x 175g sterilised jam jars (page 44)

Wash, peel and grate the horseradish, popping it into cold salted water as you go to prevent discolouration and streaming eyes. Drain well, pat dry and pack into small jars, filling two-thirds full, and adding 1 teaspoon salt, ½ teaspoon sugar and a piece of chilli to each jar. Cover with cold vinegar. Seal and label.

To use the horseradish, drain off any surplus vinegar and use in the proportions of 1 tablespoon of horseradish to 150ml cream or apple or gooseberry purée. Reserve the vinegar to serve with rich fish or add a splash to sauces and gravies.

Horseradish and Garlic Sauce

Hair-raising to say the very least! A tablespoon of this is a great addition to hefty beef casseroles and steak and kidney pies. It's also excellent strained and used with cold meats and in sandwiches, and the vinegary juice is good sprinkled discreetly on liver, bacon, sausages and other fried food. I like to use the reserved vinegar from pickled onions (or pickled walnuts if you have them) for this recipe, but if you haven't tried this recipe yet, then use 100ml good spiced vinegar mixed with 100ml balsamic vinegar or 200ml hot spiced vinegar instead.

MAKES 1 X 750G JAR

100g fresh horseradish

100g garlic

100g ground mixed spice

1 small cinnamon stick

1 teaspoon celery seeds

150ml malt vinegar

150ml soy sauce

200ml Pickled Onions vinegar (page 86)

1 x 750g sterilised jam jar (page 44)

Scrub and clean the horseradish. Peel the garlic. Finely mince the horseradish and garlic together in a mincer or food processor.

Put the mixed spice, cinnamon, celery seeds and malt vinegar into a pan and boil together, remove from the heat and cover, then leave to get cold.

Remove the cinnamon stick from the cooled vinegar and mix all the remaining ingredients together with the vinegar. Pot, seal and label.

Shake every day for 1 month. Then leave for at least 1 month before using.

MARROW

Although marrows come from a diverse family that gives us squash, pumpkins, melons, gourds, cucumbers and courgettes, we are more familiar with the long, fat, green or green and yellow, stripy vegetable, which sprawls accommodatingly on compost heaps and spare ground in allotments.

Few people grow the lovely ornamental squash, such as custard marrow or crookneck squash, which make wonderful eating. Another delicious variety that is gaining in popularity is the spaghetti squash, which has masses of golden buttery, curly pulp that, with a good sauce, makes a meal in itself.

However, the marrow that we are more concerned with is the common or garden variety, which can appear in glut proportions in the late summer and is an excellent bulk vegetable for eking out precious fruit and more expensive vegetables when making jams, chutneys and pickles. The best marrows to use for jams and chutneys are fully matured with hard skin and golden pulp. The smaller marrows are best for pickles because they retain their firmness. Always peel and seed your marrow before weighing, otherwise the results may be disastrous. It is advisable to steam or stand the prepared marrow overnight before adding to the pan to ensure that the cubes are not rubbery.

Courgettes, which are sometimes referred to as baby marrows, also work very well in most chutney and pickle recipes. You should be able to buy marrow relatively cheaply in season, especially from markets, local produce shops and village fêtes. Do not be conned into paying the inflated commercial prices asked by supermarkets.

Marrow and Ginger Jam

As it has no pectin, nor acid content, marrow benefits from the use of commercial pectin. Use this recipe as a basis for experimenting with your own additions, for example, substituting chopped crystallised angelica for the ginger gives a warm, mellow flavour, and chopped crystallised pineapple, orange peel or apricots will make a fruitier jam (omit the ginger when using these alternatives).

MAKES 6 X 375G JARS

1kg white granulated sugar, warmed (page 17)

1kg peeled, deseeded and diced marrow

2 lemons

50g dried root ginger, bruised

100g crystallised ginger

250ml bottle of commercial pectin

small muslin bag for spices

6 x 375g sterilised jam jars (page 44)

Put the prepared marrow into a large pan with 150ml water. Grate the zest from the lemons. Squeeze the juice from the lemons. Place the lemon zest and the bruised root ginger, tied in a muslin bag, in the pan. Cover and simmer for 20 minutes.

Finely chop the preserved ginger and add it to the pan with the lemon juice and the warmed sugar, stirring well until the sugar has dissolved. Bring to a full boil for 2 minutes, then remove the pan from the heat and discard the muslin bag. Stir in the pectin and skim and stir for 1 minute. Cool before potting. Seal and label when cold.

Keep for at least 1 week before using.

The Colonel's Fruit Chutney

The colonel was a customer on my market stall – he became addicted to this chutney, which I had devised especially for him. It's a very rich, fruity chutney, which is mind-bendingly hot, so if you prefer a milder flavour, reduce the amount of cayenne. This is an excellent way to use up all the odds and ends at the end of the season, particularly windfall apples and pears. If you use white sugar and vinegar, the chutney will be a very yellow colour. If you prefer a more subtle golden brown, then substitute both vinegar and sugar for the brown varieties.

MAKES 7 X 375G JARS

1kg peeled, deseeded and diced marrow

25g sea salt

1kg cooking apples

1kg hard winter or Conference pears

250g onions

350g yellow sultanas

2 teaspoons plain flour

2 teaspoons mustard powder

2 tablespoons cayenne pepper

2 tablespoons turmeric

2 tablespoons ground ginger

1 litre white malt vinegar

500g white granulated sugar

7 x 375g sterilised jam jars (page 44)

Put the peeled, deseeded and diced marrow into a colander, sprinkle with the salt, cover with a weighted plate and leave to drain overnight.

The next day, rinse the salted marrow and shake it dry;

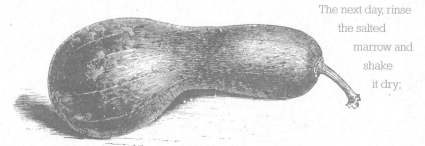

place in a steamer and cook until soft.

Wash, peel, core and chop the fruit. Peel and chop the onions. Chop or mince the sultanas. The fruit and onions can be chopped in a food processor for a finer mixture, if you prefer (and this is much easier on you!).

Mash the marrow well and put it in a pan with the fruit and onions and 150ml water. Simmer gently until the mixture is soft.

Combine the flour and spices in a bowl and mix with a little of the vinegar to make a smooth paste. Add this to the pan with half the vinegar, stir very well and simmer until thick. Dissolve the sugar in the remaining vinegar and stir into the pan. Simmer for 40 minutes until a thick, smooth consistency is reached. Pot, seal and label.

Keep for at least 1 month before using.

Tangy Marrow Chutney

An excellent chutney studded with candied orange to give an unusual, but very delicious, flavour. It is particularly good with light 'sour' cheeses like Caerphilly and Lancashire, especially when accompanied by a crusty home-baked loaf.

MAKES 4 X 375G JARS

1kg peeled, deseeded and diced marrow

25g sea salt

225g onions

225g hard cooking or eating apples

115g sultanas

50g candied orange peel

600ml malt vinegar

3 teaspoons ground ginger

½ teaspoon cayenne pepper

225g white granulated or soft brown sugar

4 x 375g sterilised jam jars (page 44)

Put the prepared marrow in a colander, sprinkle with the salt, cover with a weighted plate and leave overnight.

The next day, drain and rinse the marrow. Peel and chop the onions. Wash, peel, core and chop the apples. Chop the sultanas and peel.

Pour half the vinegar into a pan and add all the ingredients, except the sugar, cooking gently until soft. Dissolve the sugar in the remaining vinegar and add this to the pan, stirring well. Bring to the boil and simmer for about 1 hour until thick and smooth. Pot, seal and label.

Keep for at least 1 month before using.

MUSHROOMS

There are few pleasures quite so satisfying as discovering a gleaming patch of white mushroom caps sunk into dew-drenched tussocky grass, and the joy of picking wild mushrooms, taking them home and cooking them for breakfast, is a joy almost unsurpassed. A word of warning though, never pick mushrooms, ceps or fungi without knowledgeable advice. In France, during the fungi gathering season, inspectors visit every market to view the 'mushrooms' in their brown paper bags or sturdy baskets to ensure that there is nothing lethal for sale amongst those delightful stalls set out with this local produce. The dew-fresh earthy odour of mushrooms is the wonderful smell of autumn – please make sure that it is not your last. When you are out and about on a mushroom hunt, discard any with a greenish tinge or that have white gills or warts or that stain on peeling.

Field Mushrooms

Flat with dark brown gills or slightly domed with browny pink gills, these make excellent ketchups and give a rich, full flavour to sauces, soups and savouries. They can also be dried very satisfactorily. Field mushrooms that are either too mature or picked late in the day, should be well examined as they often have wormy inhabitants and should be discarded.

Horse mushrooms

Much larger, these mushrooms smell slightly of almonds. Although they dry very well, they have a very strong flavour and, if eaten in any quantity, can make you feel queasy.

Commercial Button Mushrooms

These do not have anything like the flavour of wild mushrooms, but they are easily available, they do pickle amazingly well and are extremely good as hors d'oeuvre. Do not wash wild mushrooms

because they will become flaccid when cooked. If they are freshly picked, just remove any dirt and wipe them with a damp cloth.

Mushroom Ketchup

This is an all-purpose ketchup with considerable punch. Although the alcoholic extras are not strictly necessary, I think they add a certain something to the brew.

MAKES 1 X 600ML BOTTLE

1kg field mushrooms or large flat ones from the greengrocer

75g sea salt

1 large shallot

1 large garlic clove

300ml malt vinegar

1 teaspoon pickling spice

¼ teaspoon grated nutmeg

pinch of cayenne pepper

red wine, port or brandy

1 x 600ml sterilised bottle with cork (page 44)

Wipe the mushrooms clean, peel if necessary, remove the stalks and examine for any damage, keeping all those that are good and putting them with the caps. Break up by hand and put into an earthenware casserole, layered with the salt. Cover and leave overnight. Some methods advocate longer, but I have never found this to be necessary.

Peel and chop the shallot and garlic and put them into a pan with all the remaining ingredients, except the alcohol. Bring to the boil and boil for 2 minutes, cover and leave to get cold.

The next day, preheat the oven to 100–120°C/gas mark ½. Rinse the mushrooms briefly, shake in a colander and mash well. Return them to the cleaned casserole with the prepared vinegar, cover and pop in the oven for 30 minutes.

When the juice is quite rich and substantial, strain it through a fine nylon sieve, pressing gently to obtain a good extraction. Now measure it and for each 600ml gained, take 300ml red wine or port or 1 good tablespoon brandy. Add this to the ketchup and bottle to within 3cm of the top. Seal tightly, sterilise (see page 44–5) and label.

Keep for at least 1 month before using.

Pickled mushrooms à la Grecque

Delicious as an hors d'oeuvre or an accompanying salad dish and particularly good with fish.

MAKES 2 X 375G JARS

For the vinegar

450ml white malt or white wine vinegar

50g white granulated sugar

4 bay leaves

1 dried chilli

1 teaspoon black peppercorns

For the pickle

4 pickling onions or shallots

sea salt, for sprinkling

500g small firm button mushrooms

2 tablespoons vinegar

2 teaspoons sea salt

2 x 375g wide-necked sterilised jam jars (page 44)

Put all the ingredients for the vinegar into a pan, add 175ml water and bring to the boil. Remove from the heat, cover and leave to cool.

Peel and thinly slice the onions, place them on a dish and sprinkle well with salt; leave for 2 hours.

Wipe the mushrooms and trim the stalks. Mix 2 litres water, the 2 tablespoons vinegar and 2 teaspoons salt together in a large pan and add the mushrooms. Cover and simmer for 30 minutes.

Drain and rinse well under cold running water. Return to a pan of cold water, bring to the boil and simmer for a further 30 minutes. Meanwhile, preheat the oven to 50–70°C/gas mark ¼.

Drain the mushrooms well and rinse and drain the onions. Pack the mushrooms and onions into the jars and keep them warm by placing them in the oven.

Strain the spiced vinegar retaining the bay leaves and bring it to the boil again. Pour over the mushrooms to cover, sliding the bay leaves decoratively down the sides of the jar. Seal tightly immediately and label.

Keep for at least 2 weeks before using.

Mushroom Powder

A rounded teaspoon of this makes an excellent flavouring for stocks, brown sauces, soups and casseroles.

MAKES 4 X 100G JARS

1kg field or horse mushrooms

2 small onions

¼ teaspoon ground cloves

¼ teaspoon ground mace

¼ teaspoon ground white pepper

4 x 100g sterilised jars (page 44)

Wipe the mushrooms with a damp cloth, making sure that all the pieces, including the stalks, are clean and worm-free. Peel and chop the onions.

Preheat the oven to 50–70°C/gas mark ¼. Put all the ingredients into a heavy-based pan and shake continuously over a medium heat. Cook until the mushrooms are quite dry and brittle. Lay out on a baking tray and place in the oven overnight to dry off completely.

Either grind to a powder using a pestle and mortar or in a dry liquidiser, food processor or coffee mill. Sift through a sieve and pack into jars. Seal tightly.

Keep for 1 week in a well-sealed jar or box before using. Store in a cool, dry place well away from the damp.

MUSTARD

Mustard powder is the finely ground seed of the mustard plant, of which there are several varieties. The most commonly used seeds in making preserves are black mustard seeds (*Brassica nigra*), brown mustard seeds (*Brassica juncea*) and white mustard seeds (*Sinapis alba*). They can be used mixed together or individually. The powder achieved by grinding these small seeds is used in the familiar table mustard that accompanies roast beef and that can be an annihilator of taste if used too generously!

But the seeds are a seductive addition to the preserving pan and are synonymous with mustard pickle and piccalilli. Mustard seeds can be used to great effect in making some very exciting inventions of your own.

Here I give you two examples of homemade mustard, one hot and one sweet, using two different methods. Once you have tried them, you can experiment to your heart's content. Mustard seeds can be bought from wholefood and Indian spice stockists.

Hot Mustard

MAKES 2 X 100G JARS

50g white mustard seeds

⅛ teaspoon ground nutmeg

1 large pinch ground allspice

½ teaspoon grated horseradish

8 tablespoons white wine vinegar

ground sea salt

ground black pepper

2 x 100g sterilised jars (page 44)

Crush the mustard seeds using a pestle and mortar or food processor. Transfer the seeds to a small bowl, add the remaining ingredients and stir well. Put the mixture into a small pan and heat gently until the mixture becomes creamy. Set aside to cool. Once cold, pot, seal and label.

Leave for 1 week before using.

Sweet Mustard

MAKES 1 X 150G JAR

4 tablespoons black mustard seeds

4 tablespoons yellow mustard seeds

150ml white wine vinegar

clear honey, to taste

ground sea salt, to taste

1–2 tablespoons sunflower oil (optional)

1 x 150g sterilised jar (page 44)

Grind together the black and yellow mustard seeds until they form a paste – the small grinder attachment on a mixer is great for this purpose. Put the paste into a china basin and pour enough vinegar over them until the seeds can absorb no more, stirring well between additions.

Add honey and salt to taste – this really is a matter of personal taste for which there are no guidelines. Leave for a few days and taste again; if the mixture is too strong, add 1–2 tablespoons oil. Pot, seal and label.

Leave for 1 week before using.

Mustard Pickle and Piccalilli

Since the days of the Raj, the British people have developed a penchant for pickles. Some are tonsil-searingly, eye-wateringly hot, yet the majority are relatively mild, depending upon the sauces used. The common factors in these two pickles are mustard powder or seed and turmeric, which gives the bright golden appearance. The main difference is that the mustard pickle contains both vegetables and dried or fresh fruit, left in larger pieces and cooked in the sweetened sauce for some time. Piccalilli, however, only contains vegetables, which are cut into smaller dice. They are barely cooked and the sauce is rarely sweetened.

Preparing Vegetables for Mustard Pickle and Piccalilli

To make things easier, first here's an idea of how to prepare the fruit and veg. Try and have a good mixture of different ingredients, bearing in mind that you will need 1kg prepared veg to 100g sea salt.

Apples (hard) – peel, core and dice

Carrots – peel and dice

Cauliflower – divide into small florets

Courgettes – slice crosswise

Gherkins – slice crosswise

Green beans – string and slice crosswise

Green tomatoes – quarter and deseed

Marrows – peel, deseed and dice

Nasturtium seeds – leave whole

Peppers – deseed and small dice

Pickling cucumbers – peel and dice

Prunes and sultanas

(only for mustard pickle) – chop and

add 10 minutes before end of cooking

Radishes – cut in half

Small onions and shallots – peel and

quarter if large

For each 1kg vegetables you will need
3–4 x 375g sterilised jam jars (page 44).

Piccalilli

Lay the prepared vegetables on a
large flat dish and sprinkle each 1kg
veg with 100g sea salt, making sure
that all the layers get a good helping.
Cover and leave overnight.

The next day, put the vegetables
in a colander and rinse under cold,
running water; shake and drain very
well. Make up your chosen sauce, as
shown below, and mix the vegetables
into it while still boiling. For a soft
pickle, cook the vegetables in the
sauce for 5 minutes; for a crisper
pickle, just bring the mixture to the
boil; and for a very crisp pickle, mix

the vegetables in off the heat.

Pot in sterilised jars, seal and label.

Keep for at least 1 month before
using.

Mustard Pickle

Prepare the ingredients as for
Piccalilli, but simmer the ingredients
gently in the hot or spicy sauce for
approximately 1 hour.

Pot in sterilised jars, seal and label.

Keep for at least 1 month before
using.

Sweet Mustard Pickle

Add 100–125g white or brown sugar
to 1kg vegetables, then add it to the
mixture with the sauce and cook gently
for 1 hour.

Pot in sterilised jars (see page 44),
seal and label.

Keep for at least 1 month before using.

A Hot Sauce for Piccalilli or Mustard Pickle

You can use either brown or white
vinegar, but I think white gives the
sauce a better colour.

**MAKES ENOUGH FOR 1KG
PREPARED VEGETABLES**

2 garlic cloves

750ml malt or white malt vinegar

1 tablespoon dried red chillies

6cm piece of dried root ginger, bruised

1 tablespoon black peppercorns

1 tablespoon cornflour

1 tablespoon turmeric

1 tablespoon mustard powder

Bruise the garlic. Boil together 600ml of the vinegar, the chillies, ginger, peppercorns and bruised garlic. Remove from the heat, cover and allow to become quite cold.

Strain the spiced vinegar and mix it to a smooth paste with the cornflour, turmeric and mustard, add the remaining vinegar and continue as for the given method.

A Spicy Sauce for Piccalilli or Mustard Pickle

You can use either brown or white malt vinegar, but I think white gives the sauce a better colour.

**MAKES ENOUGH FOR 1KG
PREPARED VEGETABLES**

2 garlic cloves

25g fresh horseradish

25g shallots

2 teaspoons black peppercorns

1 teaspoon whole allspice

6 whole cloves

2 x 6cm pieces of dried root ginger

750ml malt or white malt vinegar

1 tablespoon turmeric

2 level tablespoons mustard powder

¼ teaspoon cayenne pepper

Bruise the garlic. Grate the horseradish. Peel and chop the shallots. Lightly bruise the whole spices and ginger. Put the prepared ingredients into a pan with 600ml of the vinegar and boil for 5 minutes.

Mix the remaining vinegar with the turmeric, mustard powder and cayenne pepper to form a smooth paste. Add the strained spiced vinegar and continue as for the given method.

ONIONS

The most well known and frequently used member of the allium family, which includes shallots, leeks, garlic and chives. If you have ever been left without onions in the kitchen, you will realise just how vital they are to cooking, particularly in the making of pickles and chutneys. There are five basic types of onions:

All-purpose Onion

Varies from pale gold to carmine red and is the most valuable in cooking and preserving as it keeps its flavour well. Red onions have a slightly sweeter flavour.

Spanish Onion

Large and golden, it is mild enough to be eaten raw or as a whole braised or roast vegetable. Especially useful when a recipe requires a mild onion.

Pickling Onions

Small and fast growing and not to be confused with shallots. They are ideal for pickling and excellent in preserves.

Silverskin Onions

Very small and a pure white colour. More widely available and popular on the continent than in the UK. Perfect for use as a cocktail onion and in mixed pickles.

Spring Onions

Used principally in salads and as a garnish.

Shallots

Short, stubby onions with as much as 4 separate 'cloves' within one skin or elongated ovoid banana shallots, which, on the whole, are too large for pickling. The flavour of shallots is perfect for pickling in balsamic vinegar or sherry – an expensive option compared to the good old pickled onion.

Whatever variety you are buying, make sure they are dry and firm with no mould, otherwise they are likely to be brown throughout. And finally… no-one can escape from the tell-tale aroma of second-hand onions on the breath. Chew parsley or have a strong black coffee to eradicate it.

Pickled Onions

The preparation for all onions is pretty much the same. Peel the onions, taking as little from the base and top as possible as this causes bruising and discolouration. A very good way of ensuring that the skins come off as quickly as possible whilst subduing those dreaded fumes, is to drop the onions into boiling water, leave for 1 minute, drain and dip in cold water. Peel under cold water using a very sharp, preferably stainless steel, knife to prevent discolouration. Transfer them to a bowl of cold water as you work. Drain well.

For crisp pickled onions, just lay them on a large plate and sprinkle with 50g sea salt to each 1kg onions. Cover and leave overnight. The next day, rinse well, drain and dry. I prefer this method of salting as it gives a crisp, well-seasoned result.

For a softer pickle, brine the onions by leaving them overnight in a solution of 100g sea salt to 1 litre water. Rinse, drain and dry well.

Very small onions may be peeled and packed without further preparation.

When the onions are prepared, make sure that they are absolutely dry before packing them firmly into 2x500g dry sterilised jars (see page 44) with non-metal or plastic-lined lids. Cover with either a hot or cold spiced vinegar of your choice (see opposite). A hot vinegar will give a softer pickle, whilst the cold vinegar will give you a crispy, crunchy pickle. The vinegar may be strained or left as it is – it will be hotter if the spices are left in and they will look very decorative if white vinegar is used. A handy hint if you are using white vinegar is to add a few drops of sweet almond oil to each jar to keep that pristine appearance – the tiny white silverskin onions will benefit particularly from this. White onions should be pickled in white or white wine vinegar and the following seasonings may be used: basil, nutmeg, celery seeds, chilli, chervil, rosemary or dill. Pickled onions should be left for at least 1 month before using to allow the vinegar to penetrate. Try experimenting with your own vinegars – horseradish, chilli, etc. – and never throw away the vinegar from your pickled onions as it comes in useful for salad dressings and sauces and even for sprinkling on chips!

All-purpose Hot Vinegar

You can use either brown or white malt vinegar, but white malt vinegar gives the finished result a more decorative appearance.

MAKES ENOUGH FOR 1KG PREPARED ONIONS

1.1 litres brown or white malt vinegar
2 tablespoons mustard seeds
2 tablespoons whole cloves
2 tablespoon black peppercorns
2 tablespoons whole allspice
2 tablespoons dried chillies

Boil the vinegar with the spices for 10 minutes, allow to cool and strain before using.

Produces a pickled onion that, in our household, is known as mother's little gasper!

A More Mellow Vinegar

MAKES ENOUGH FOR 1KG PREPARED ONIONS

1.1 litres white malt vinegar
a few blades mace
1 teaspoon whole cloves
bay leaves and sliced pimentos, to add to the jar

Boil the vinegar, mace and cloves together for 10 minutes and strain before using.

Pack the bay leaves and pimentos into the sterilised jar with the onions. This recipe can be adapted for shallots by using half the vinegar to half sherry or even balsamic vinegar.

Vinegar for Silverskin Onions

MAKES ENOUGH FOR 1KG PREPARED ONIONS

1 litre white wine vinegar
1 teaspoon whole cloves
1 tablespoon dried red chillies and whole fresh tarragon leaves, to add to the jar

Boil the vinegar first with the cloves for 10 minutes and leave it to get cold.

Strain the vinegar, then pack the chillies and tarragon into the jars with the onions and cover with the cold vinegar.

Vinegar for Small Pickling Onions

MAKES ENOUGH FOR 1KG PREPARED ONIONS

1 litre white malt vinegar

6 fresh or dried red chillies, halved lengthways

6cm piece of dried root ginger, sliced

1 tablespoon black peppercorns

½ teaspoon sea salt

Boil the vinegar for 5 minutes and allow it to cool.

Pack the onions into the jars, interspersing each layer with chilli, ginger, peppercorns and salt. Cover with the cold vinegar.

Sweet Pickled Onions

Either of the two above recipes can be used for sweet pickled onions by the addition of 25g white granulated sugar. Stir it into the boiling vinegar just before removing from the heat, but do make sure that it has dissolved properly.

Onion Relish

A mild relish that children like – it tastes especially good in homemade hamburgers.

MAKES 3 X 375G JARS

1kg mild onions

1 dessertspoon sea salt

1 large cooking apple

1 large red pepper

100ml white malt or cider vinegar

1 dessertspoon fresh tarragon leaves or ½ teaspoon dried tarragon

½ teaspoon ground white pepper

½ teaspoon ground mace

100g white granulated sugar

3 x 375g sterilised jam jars (page 44)

Peel the onions and either mince them or put them in a food processor and whizz until they are finely chopped. Cover with the salt and leave to stand overnight, turning the mixture over several times. The next day, drain them thoroughly to remove excess liquid.

Peel and core the apple. Deseed the pepper. Put both through the mincer or processor. Place all the ingredients, except the sugar, in a pan and cook gently until soft and nicely mixed. Add the sugar, stirring well to make sure

it is dissolved, bring to the boil, then simmer for a further 20 minutes. Pot, seal and label.

Keep for at least 2 weeks before using.

Italian Mixed Vegetable Pickle

This is an excellent method of preserving a variety of vegetables in a mild vinegar for use in salads or, quite possibly, hors d'oeuvre. These pretty pickles do not last for an indefinite time, but as they usually get gobbled up quite quickly, this should not be a problem. One particular village in Italy has pickle-making down to a fine art. The residents build small pictures of churches and the countryside using the vegetables placed with infinite patience and artistic flair within each jar.

First, prepare a selection of vegetables, as on page 88, bearing in mind that the amount of spiced vinegar is enough to pickle 1kg prepared veg. Blanch nasturtium seeds and radish pods by adding 25g salt to 1 litre water, bringing to the boil, adding the seeds or pods and withdrawing the pan from the heat, leaving for 5 minutes and then draining.

Carrots
Peeled and cut into fine slices
Cauliflower
Divide into small florets
Small Gherkins
Left whole
Small Courgettes
Unpeeled, thickly sliced crosswise
Small Green Tomatoes
Pierced with a needle and left whole
Nasturtium Seeds
Blanched in brine
Peppers
Cut into short thick strips
Radish pods
Blanched in brine
Small Runner or
Haricot Beans
Left whole
Silverskin, Pickling or
Small Shallot Onions
Peeled
Dried Chilli, a shred of
lemon peel, a bay leaf or a
sprig of herbs, for decoration

For each 1kg vegetables, you will need 2 x 1-litre sterilised wide-necked jars (see page 44). It is important to use jars with a wide neck otherwise it is almost impossible to pack the vegetables, and even more impossible to retrieve them.

Prepare the vegetables and pack them into the sterilised jars. Cover with the cold strained white vinegar of your choice (see below). Decorate the filled jar with a dried chilli, a shred of lemon, a bay leaf or a sprig of herbs. Seal and label.

Keep for at least 1 week before using. Store in the fridge once opened and use within 2 months. The vegetables can be salted in the same way as pickled onions to make them last longer, but this does tend to make them go limp.

A Mild Vinegar

MAKES ENOUGH FORT 1KG
PREPARED VEGETABLES

50g shallots

1 litre white malt vinegar

25g mustard seeds

1 tablespoon pickling spice

Peel and chop the shallots and put with the remaining ingredients into a saucepan. Bring to the boil and boil hard for 5 minutes. Remove from the heat, cover and leave for 2 hours. Strain before using.

A Hotter Vinegar

If you prefer a hotter vinegar, then add 2 chopped garlic cloves and 2 dried red chillies to the vinegar before boiling as opposite.

Either of the two vinegars suggested for pickling small white or silverskin onions (see pages 85–6) are also pretty perfect.

Nun's Sauce

This is almost certainly based on one of the very ancient sauces used by Romans in the days of Caesar. I cannot believe, though, that the good sisters required such hair-raising additions to their diet! Perhaps they saved the sauce for visiting bishops? This is an excellent addition to soups, sauces or a good beef casserole.

MAKES 6 X 150ML BOTTLES

3 garlic cloves

3 shallots

1 tablespoon preserved anchovies (from a tin or jar)

1 tablespoon cayenne pepper

1 tablespoon soft brown sugar

1.1 litres malt vinegar

1 teaspoon whole cloves

1.5-litre sterilised jar (page 44) with a tightly fitting lid (for authenticity, a stone jar should be used)

muslin cloth for straining

6 x 150ml sterilised bottles with corks (page 44)

Peel and chop the garlic and shallots and pound them to a paste with the anchovies. Mix the cayenne pepper and the sugar to a smooth paste with a little of the vinegar. Crumble the cloves. Put all the ingredients in the jar. Seal tightly and leave for 1 month, shaking the jar day and night.

Strain through a muslin cloth. Transfer to sterilised bottles, seal with corks and label. Keep for 1 week before using.

PEPPER

Although once a rarity in northern Europe, the pepper, or capsicum, is now a familiar vegetable in our shops. Sweet peppers range in colour from pale olive green, glossy viridian, yellow, orange, scarlet and crimson and their taste is mild, sweet and very distinctive, although this can vary. Some peppers have thick chunky skin, whilst others, particularly the long, tapering varieties, have a much thinner skin and are considerably sweeter and sometimes quite hot. The smallest and most virulent varieties of capsicum are the chilli peppers.

Peppers and chilli peppers are available throughout the year. As a rough guide, it's worth remembering approximately 4 firm sweet peppers will weigh 450g.

Red Pepper Relish

A pleasant sweet relish, which I always enjoy with barbecued meats.

MAKES 3 X 375G JARS

6 red peppers

1 fresh red chilli

2 large white onions

4 garlic cloves

300ml white malt vinegar

2 teaspoons sea salt

2 teaspoons freshly ground black pepper

275g white granulated sugar

3 x 375g sterilised jam jars (page 44)

Halve and deseed the peppers and chilli and finely chop them. Cover and leave to one side.

Peel and either whizz or cut the onions and garlic very finely. Place the onions and garlic in a pan and cook them with the vinegar and salt and pepper until soft. Add the peppers and chilli and continue to cook until the peppers have softened.

Add the sugar to the pan, stirring well until it has dissolved and bring gently to the boil. Simmer for about 40 minutes until thick and soft.

Pot, seal and label.

Keep for 2 weeks before using.

Nick's Great Ratatouille Mixture

Nick is a great and imaginative cook who occasionally overbuys, and this is the result of one of his very good experiments – a hot, tasty and cheerful chutney, which goes well with everything. If this looks like a terrifyingly large amount of chutney, reduce the ingredients by half.

MAKES 10 X 375G JARS

1kg red and green peppers

1kg red tomatoes

500g aubergines

2 teaspoons sea salt

150g fresh green and red chillies

500g onions

3 large garlic cloves

2 teaspoons paprika

2 teaspoons mustard seeds

750ml white malt vinegar

1 teaspoon cayenne pepper

250g white granulated sugar

10 x 375g sterilised jam jars (page 44)

Remove the seeds and pith from the peppers and chop the flesh. Skin and chop the tomatoes. Wash the aubergines and cut into small pieces, sprinkle them with 1 teaspoon of the salt and lay them in a colander with a plate on top whilst you get on with the rest. (This helps to soften them and gets rid of any bitter juices.) Shred the chillies. Peel and chop the onions. Peel the garlic and put it into a pestle and mortar with the remaining salt, the paprika and mustard seeds; grind away merrily until fairly well crushed.

Put the tomatoes into a large pan with the onions, the salty garlic mixture and half the vinegar and just simmer gently for about 40 minutes until the onions become soft. Shake the aubergines free of salt and put them with all the other ingredients into the pan of tomatoes, bring gently to the boil,

stirring constantly, and then simmer for approximately 2 hours or until the mixture is soft, thick and pungent.

Pot, seal and label.

Keep for 3 months before using.

Peperoni Tricolore

Tasty and crunchy and a terrific addition to salads. They will go soft if kept for much more than 4 weeks, but can be kept in the fridge, especially once opened.

MAKES 1 X 1 LITRE JAR

1 red pepper

1 green pepper

1 yellow pepper

2 carrots

2 stalks celery

1 small fennel bulb

a few fennel and celery leaves

sea salt

600ml cider or white malt vinegar

1 teaspoon celery seeds

1 teaspoon dill seeds

2 teaspoons white granulated sugar

1 small garlic clove

2 bay leaves

1 x 1-litre sterilised wide-necked preserving jar (page 44)

Seal tightly and keep refrigerated once opened.

Keep for 1 week before using. It is best kept in the fridge once opened.

Pepper and Tomato Chutney

A traditional chutney with hints of Eastern flavours from the spices and sultanas.

Keeping each vegetable on a separate plate, wash and deseed the peppers and cut into small squares. Peel the carrots and cut into matchsticks. Wash the celery and fennel and cut into strips. Sprinkle all the vegetables, including the fennel and celery leaves, with salt. Cover and leave for several hours.

In the meantime, boil the vinegar with the remaining ingredients for 5 minutes, then cover and leave for several hours to get cold.

Drain the vegetables, rinse and pat dry, keeping them separate. Pack them into the jar in alternate layers, infiltrating the bay leaves, celery and fennel fronds artistically amongst them. Discard the garlic, give the vinegar a good stir and pour it over the vegetables to cover.

MAKES 6 X 375G JARS

450g Spanish onions

1 large garlic clove

1kg red peppers

2 large juicy tomatoes

2 tablespoons olive oil

250g sultanas

1 teaspoon ground ginger

1 teaspoon ground cloves

1 teaspoon allspice

1 teaspoon ground cinnamon

200g white granulated sugar

450ml red wine vinegar

6 x 375g sterilised jam jars (page 44)

Peel and finely chop the onions and garlic. Deseed the peppers and cut them into thin rounds. Skin (see page 65) and chop the tomatoes.

Pour the oil into a large pan, heat gently and add the onions, garlic, peppers and tomatoes. Sauté very carefully over a low heat for 15 minutes and do not allow to burn. Add the sultanas and spices and then gradually add the sugar, a little at a time, testing for sweetness as you go. Add the vinegar and simmer, uncovered, on a low heat for 3–4 hours, stirring occasionally.

Pot, seal and label.

Keep for 6 months before using.

TOMATO

The tomato, or tomatl, from Peru, travelled through South America to Europe where the Italians christened this fiery fruit pomo d'oro, or golden apple. In Spain it gained another name: pomo de Mori, or Moors' apple, and thence on to France where, not unsurprisingly, it was christened the pomme d'amour, or love apple! When it reached Britain, however, it was viewed with great suspicion as being a 'cold fruit' and a member of the nightshade family. Not until the 20th century was this fear more or less eradicated and the tomatoes' valuable vitamin C content and culinary uses appreciated.

Green tomatoes are as good as red tomatoes in making preserves, but if you wish to force a few green tomatoes to turn red, then pop them into a brown paper bag and leave them in a dark airing cupboard. Tomatoes, like many other seasonal fruit and vegetables, ripen in yours and everyone else's gardens at the same time, therefore farmers' markets and local produce stalls should be selling them more reasonably priced – so make the most of it. When buying tomatoes, remember they reduce considerably when cooked, so make allowances for this.

Tomato Marmalade

Blood oranges give a good colour to this delicious Spanish recipe. If you can't get hold of them, any sweet oranges will do. It is best eaten as a sweet preserve, but it's also nice with meat and cheese.

MAKES 4 X 375G JARS

1kg ripe tomatoes

6 blood oranges

3 lemons

1kg white granulated sugar, warmed
(page 17)

4 x 375g sterilised jam jars (page 44)

Skin the tomatoes (see page 65).
Wash the oranges and lemons and
take thin peelings from them with a
potato peeler. Cut the rind into hair-
thin strips and put these into a small
pan with a little water, bring to the
boil and then simmer for 15 minutes.

Remove the pith from the citrus
fruit. Put the tomatoes through a
coarse mincer or food processor with
the orange and lemon flesh, making
sure that you catch the juice and
discard the pips. Place this mushy
mixture into a pan with the juices.
Drain the softened rind and add it
to the pan. Bring to the boil. Cover
and simmer for approximately 20
minutes, uncover and boil rapidly for
10 minutes.

The boiling should cause the
mixture to reduce. Measure the pulp
with a measuring jug and for each
600ml, weigh out 450g sugar. Return
the pulp to the pan, heat gently and
add the warmed sugar, stirring
continuously. Bring to the boil and
boil hard until a set is obtained (see
page 36). Pot, seal and label.

Keep for 1 week before using. This
will last for the same time as a jam,
but should be stored in the fridge
once opened.

Green Tomato Jam with Limes

This has a glorious greeny gold
colour and a unique taste, rather like
a delicious mixture of green salad
and limes. It can be used as a jam,
but is also fantastic with delicate
cheeses, salami and ham.

MAKES 3 X 375G JARS

1kg small green tomatoes

750g white granulated sugar

2 limes

1 vanilla pod

3 x 375g sterilised jam jars (page 44)

Wash, wipe and slice the tomatoes
thinly. Place in a bowl in layers with the
sugar and leave to macerate for
24 hours.

Wipe the limes and slice them very

thinly, removing the pips but catching the juices. Place all the ingredients in a pan and bring gently to the boil. Skim and then continue to simmer very gently, stirring continuously, until the jam is golden, cooked and a set is obtained (see page 36); this will take approximately 2 hours.

Remove the vanilla pod and allow the jam to cool before potting.

Stir, pot, seal and label when cold.

This is ready to eat as soon as it has set and cooled.

Red Tomato Honey

An unusual preserve for all those devotees of peanut butter and tomato jelly sandwiches! It is also an excellent spread in wholemeal sandwiches with cream cheese.

MAKES 3 X 375G JARS

1kg ripe red tomatoes

3 lemons

white granulated sugar, warmed (page 17)

125ml commercial pectin

3 x 375g sterilised jam jars (page 44)

Wash and roughly chop the tomatoes. Grate the rind from the lemons and squeeze the juice.

Put the tomatoes into a large pan with the lemon rind and cook until there is no surplus moisture, but taking care not to burn. Put into a liquidiser (do remember to fasten the lid securely, tomato leaves a terrible stain on white ceilings!) and process, then sieve. If you do not have a liquidiser, then just sieve. Measure the purée and for each 600ml, weigh out 450g warmed sugar.

Return the purée to the pan with the lemon juice, heat gently and add the warmed sugar, stirring well until it has dissolved. Bring to the boil and boil for 2 minutes. Remove from the heat and stir in the pectin, stir well and return to the boil for 2 more minutes. Pot, seal and label.

Ready to eat as soon as you like.

Fruity Tomato Sauce

A phenomenal tomato ketchup – quite different from Mr Heinz's! As with any tomato sauce, this goes well with macaroni cheese, cauliflower cheese and similar dishes. It is also pretty good with cold pork and chicken.

MAKES 2 X 500ML BOTTLES

1kg ripe red tomatoes

2 large pears

2 large peaches

2 large onions

1 red pepper

1 tablespoon whole allspice

750ml white or brown malt vinegar

1 tablespoon sea salt

500g white granulated sugar

small muslin bag for spices

2 x 500ml sterilised wide-necked bottles (page 44)

Skin the tomatoes (see page 65). Peel the pears, peaches and onions. Core the pears, remove the peach stones and deseed the pepper. Chop the fruit and vegetables into small dice.

Put the fruit and veg in the large pan with the allspice tied into a muslin bag. Add the vinegar and salt and bring slowly to the boil, stirring occasionally to prevent burning. Boil until the fruity mixture is very soft. Remove the spice bag.

Now you can either put the whole mixture into a blender and whizz to form a fine pulp or put the mixture through a sieve. Return the pulp to the pan, heat gently and add the sugar, stirring continuously until it has dissolved. Cook until the mixture is thick. Allow to cool a little before bottling. Seal tightly and label.

Keep for 1 month before using.

Tomato Chutney

A good, unusual chutney with a full, strong flavour – the combination of sun-dried tomatoes and dark brown sugar gives it a special richness.

MAKES 4 X 375G JARS

250g sun-dried tomatoes

1 dessertspoon coriander seeds

1 dessertspoon mustard seeds

900g red tomatoes

2 red peppers

2 red chillies

4 onions

4 fat garlic cloves

600ml white malt vinegar

1 dessertspoon sea salt

250g soft dark brown sugar

4 x 375g sterilised jam jars (see page 44)

Leave the dried tomatoes to soak in just enough warm water to cover for 20 minutes. Heat a non-stick frying pan over a medium heat and toast the coriander and mustard seeds, stirring constantly, until lightly coloured.

Skin and chop the fresh tomatoes (see page 65). Deseed and finely chop the peppers and chillies, and peel and chop the onion and garlic. Put the dried tomatoes and their soaking water, chillies, onions and garlic into a blender and give it a good whizz. Grind the spices using a pestle and mortar.

Put all of the tomato mixture and spices into a large pan with the vinegar and salt. Bring gently to the boil and cook until the mixture is soft. Add the sugar, stirring well until it has dissolved, bring gently to the boil and boil until the chutney is thick and soft. Pot, seal and label.

Keep for 1 month before using.

Fruity Green Tomato Chutney

A well-flavoured traditional recipe – great to make at the end of the summer when the last of the home-grown tomatoes stubbornly refuse to ripen!

MAKES 8 X 375G JARS

1kg green tomatoes

500g onions

100g shallots

2 large garlic cloves

750g peeled, deseeded and diced marrow

25g sea salt

500g soft light brown sugar

750g windfall apples

125g raisins

50g crystallised ginger, chopped

4 teaspoons dried red chillies

4 teaspoons whole cloves

4 teaspoons black peppercorns

2 tablespoons mustard seeds

25g dried root ginger

900ml malt vinegar

small muslin bag for spices

8 x 375g sterilised jam jars (page 44)

Chop the tomatoes, peel and chop the onions, shallots and garlic. Put all the prepared vegetables, including the marrow, in a large dish or bowl and sprinkle with the salt and sugar. Leave overnight, turning several times.

The next day, peel, core and chop the apples and put them into a large pan with the vegetables, then add the raisins and crystallised ginger. Bruise the spices and root ginger and tie them into the muslin bag, then add this to the pan with the vinegar and bring gently to the boil, stirring well. Simmer until thick and soft – approximately 2 hours.

Remove and discard the muslin bag. Pot, seal and label.

Keep for 1 month before using.

Hot Tomato Pickle

A spicy pickle that certainly has a little kick to it! Great with sausages – try it on hot dogs instead of ketchup or mustard.

MAKES 4 X 375G JARS

1kg green tomatoes

500g cooking apples

2 large onions

2 teaspoons sea salt

100g raisins

1.1 litres white malt vinegar

225g white granulated sugar

25g mustard seeds

1 teaspoon ground ginger

¼ teaspoon cayenne pepper

4 x 375g sterilised jam jars (page 44)

Wash and thinly slice the tomatoes. Peel, core and thinly slice the apples. Peel and thinly slice the onions.

Lay all these on a large plate and sprinkle with the salt. Cover and leave overnight.

The next day, drain off the salty liquid, rinse and drain the fruit and onions well. Put all the ingredients into a pan. Bring slowly to the boil, stirring well, and then simmer very gently for at least 1 hour until soft. Pot, seal and label.

Keep for 1 month before using.

Tomato and Horseradish Relish

The fieriness of this relish can be altered by the amount of horseradish used. It's a very hot, very tasty addition to cold meat sandwiches.

MAKES 5 X 175G JARS

300ml vinegar

1 tablespoon pickling spice

1kg firm red tomatoes

1 large cooking apple

1 medium onion

2 teaspoons sea salt

½ teaspoon cayenne pepper

3 tablespoons grated fresh horseradish

225g white granulated sugar

5 x 175g sterilised jam jars (page 44)

Put the vinegar and pickling spice into a small pan, cover and simmer gently for 10 minutes.

Skin and chop the tomatoes (see page 65). Peel, core and chop the apple. Peel and chop the onion. Put all of these ingredients together in a large pan and cook very carefully, without burning, until thick and pulpy, stirring frequently to make sure that it does not catch.

Strain the hot vinegar and add it to the pan with the salt and cayenne. Cook until thick and soft. Add the horseradish and sugar to the pan and bring to the boil, stirring constantly. Boil for 15 minutes. Pot, seal and label.

Keep for 2 weeks before using.

FRUIT

APPLES

The golden fruit of the Gods or the dream of Johnny Appleseed, apples have enjoyed unsurpassed popularity since the known beginnings of time. From those first scrubby little crab apples have emerged the widely available and popular Braeburn, Cox's Orange Pippin and Granny Smith. In times past there was an apple to suit all occasions and every taste. Apples with names redolent of the countryside and the men who grew them – Peasgood Nonesuch, Pearmain, Ashmead's Colonel, Egremont Russet, Bramley's Seedling and Grenadier, the last two being excellent examples of good cooking apples. These wonderful varieties of apple are still available, but they have to be searched for outside the limitations of the supermarket. Farmers' markets are a good source of traditional and old-fashioned fruits of all kind. Windfalls can also be garnered from friendly gardeners who will frequently leave boxes of surplus fruit by the roadside rather than see it rot, and these are the fruit that are most economical for making preserves.

Apples are high in pectin, so they are an excellent basis for other fruit, especially soft fruits with a low setting potential. They can also be used to bulk up more expensive ingredients in both jams and pickles as their flavour is never overwhelming.

Any type of apple can be used for preserving, although cooking apples will become soft and fluffy, which may not necessarily be what you want. Eating apples and hard green windfalls tend to give you crunchy bits with plenty of bite. The choice is yours and remember that pots and pots of plain apple jam will give you a multitude of winter puddings and cakes and a great deal of pleasure, whilst the tarted-up little numbers will serve you even better.

FRUIT

Apple Jam

This is a good basic jam, useful for tarts and pies. It is also a jam with which you can experiment – see the variations below.

MAKES 6 X 375G JARS

1kg windfall or cooking apples

2 lemons

1kg white granulated sugar, warmed (page 17)

large muslin bag, for peelings

6 x 375g sterilised jam jars (page 44)

Wash, peel and core the apples, discarding any less than perfect pieces and small livestock! Chop the fruit roughly and pare the rind from the lemons with a potato peeler. Do not discard the peelings, but tie them into a muslin bag with the lemon peel.

Put the fruit and muslin bag into a preserving pan with 300ml water, bring gently to the boil, then reduce the heat and simmer gently for about 40 minutes until the fruit is soft although, unless you are using only cooking apples, the fruit should not have turned mushy.

Squeeze the juice from the lemons. When the fruit is cooked, remove the muslin bag from the pan, giving it a good squeeze, stir in the warmed sugar and lemon juice and bring gently to the boil, stirring constantly until the sugar has dissolved. Bring to the boil and boil until a set is obtained (see page 36), watching like a hawk to ensure that the jam does not burn. Pot, seal and label immediately.

This preserve can be eaten the next day. Store in a cool, dry place.

Variations

Apple and Lemon Jam

Follow the basic recipe as above, but when the sugar is added, add the grated rind and the juice of 2 extra lemons.

Apple and Orange Jam

Follow the basic recipe as above, but substitute the grated rind and juice of 2 large oranges for the lemon rind and juice.

Spiced Apple Jam

Whole cloves, cinnamon, ginger, mace, cardamom and allspice can be added to the bag of peelings, either individually or in a mixture, to give a zing.

FRUIT

Apple and Ginger Jam

Add a good piece of root ginger to the bag of peelings and stir 25–50g of chopped preserved ginger into the cooked jam.

Candied Fruit Apple Jam

Chopped candied angelica or pineapple also make marvellous additions to this plain jam and transform it into the perfect filling for flans. Add to the jam at the end of cooking and leave it to cool, give it a good stir before potting to ensure an even dispersal. Seal when quite cold.

Apple and Dried Apricot Conserve

A lovely gentle jam, which is extremely tasty on good brown toast or in a homemade pie.

MAKES 5 X 375G JARS

450g dried apricots

1kg cooking apples

1 lemon

1 lime

1kg white granulated sugar

100g Demerara sugar

5 x 375g sterilised jars (page 44)

Wash the apricots and leave them to soak overnight in 750ml water.

The next day, wash, peel, core and slice the apples and place them in a pan. Drain the apricots, reserving as much of the water as you can, but minus the grotty bits at the bottom, and chop them roughly. Add them to the pan of apples with the water. Cover and simmer for about 1 hour until soft.

Grate the rind and squeeze the juice from the lemon and lime and put this into the pan of cooking fruit. Warm through and add the sugars, stirring constantly until dissolved. Bring to the boil and boil until a set is obtained (see page 36). Allow to cool a little and give it a good stir. Pot, seal and label when cold.

This conserve can be eaten the next day.

Apple Jelly

Children like this jelly stirred into a milk pudding, but it is just as good on bread and butter and also a treat on pancakes and waffles. The savoury jellies make a pleasant change in sandwiches, especially for children who do not like chutney.

Preserving sugar is, without doubt, the best sugar to use for jelly making because it gives better, clearer colour and transparency and there will be less scum after cooking.

This is the basic recipe, but for exciting variations there are some delightful herb and spice jellies to be made by the simple addition of a few little extras (see below). This basic method can also be used to great effect with 1kg gooseberries, red or white currants, oranges and lemons.

MAKES 4 X 375G JARS

1kg cooking or good-quality windfall or crab apples

white preserving sugar, warmed (page 17)

muslin or jelly bag

4 x 375g sterilised jam jars (page 44)

Wash the fruit and chop roughly. Simmer with 1.5 litres water until very soft and then turn the pulpy fruit into a muslin bag laid over a colander placed over a deep bowl. (This arrangement is a very good alternative to a professional jelly bag.) Tie up the bag and hang it above the bowl. Leave it to drip overnight and do not prod, poke or squeeze the bag, no matter how tempting. If you do so you will cause the jelly to become cloudy.

The next day, measure the juice gained and for each 600ml, weigh out 450g warmed sugar. Heat the apple juice gently, stir in the sugar and keep stirring until the sugar has dissolved. Boil rapidly until a set is obtained (see page 36). Skim, pot, label and seal.

This preserve can be eaten the next day. Store in a cool, dry place.

Variations

Herb Jellies

For the most attractive effect in both flavour and appearance, it is best to make a light, clear jelly, which will give the most benefit of your chosen herbs.

Take a bunch of fresh bright herbs picked before the sun is at its height. Divide the bunch in half and wash and dry well. The first half of the bunch goes into the gently stewing fruit. The second half is chopped and added to the jelly just before potting, but remember to allow the jelly to cool a little, stirring well to disperse the leaves before pouring into the jars. The jelly must be quite cold before sealing.

With some herbs, an attractive

spray can be popped into the jar of half-set jelly instead of chopping the herb up – this looks particularly good with rosemary, thyme, hyssop, sage or scented geranium leaves – and again the jelly must be cold before sealing.

Spiced Jellies

These are so easy to make! Take the whole spices of your choice, such as some ginger, allspice, cloves, cinnamon or, to be really different, cardamom seeds, and add them to the pan of stewing fruit where they will impart their delicious perfume.

Apple and Quince Jelly

A deep golden jelly with a unique perfumed taste. Absolutely excellent with game and cold meats.

MAKES 8 X 175G JARS

1kg apples

1kg quince

2 large lemons

white preserving sugar, warmed (page 17)

muslin or jelly bag

8 x 175g sterilised jam jars (page 44)

Wash and roughly chop the apples and quince. Place in a preserving pan with just enough water to cover. Bring slowly to the boil and then simmer until the fruit has become soft and pulpy. If it looks like drying out, then add a little more water because you will need as much juice as possible and quince absorbs water quite rapidly, but do not overdo it otherwise you will not achieve a set. Turn the fruit out into a muslin or jelly bag or equivalent (see Apple jelly, opposite page), tie the fruit securely in place and hang the bag above the bowl. Leave the fruit to drip into the bowl overnight. Do not be tempted to prod it as this will lead to a cloudy jelly.

The next day, squeeze the juice from the lemons. Measure the apple and quince juice and for every 600ml of juice, weigh out 500g warmed sugar. Return the apple and quince juice to the clean pan with the lemon juice and bring to the boil, add the sugar and stir well until it has dissolved. Bring back to the boil, skim to remove the scum and then continue at a shivering boil until a set is obtained (see page 36). Skim and pour into jars. Leave to become quite cold before sealing and labelling.

Keep overnight before using.

Crab Apple and Rowan Jelly

Rowan (or mountain ash) berries have a deliciously tart flavour, which will be mellowed by cooking with crab apples. This jelly is a favourite accompaniment to venison and game. Both crab apple and rowan trees are parkland favourites and it should not be difficult to find some fruit going begging, but do leave some for the birds to enjoy too!

MAKES 8 X 175G JARS

1kg crab apples

1kg rowan berries

white preserving sugar, warmed (page 17)

2 lemons

muslin or jelly bag

8 x 175g sterilised jars (page 44)

Wash and roughly chop the apples. Place in a large preserving pan and cover with water. Cook until mushy and soft. You may well have to add a little more water or get to work with the old elbow grease and a wooden potato masher, as crab apples can be quite notorious in the length of time they take to cook.

In the meantime, remove the rowan berries from their stalks, this is best done through the tines of a fork, and wash them. Place in a separate pan and add 500ml water. Cook until they are just beginning to soften and then pour the contents of the pan into the crab apples. Bring to the boil and stir well. Cook for a further 5 minutes. Turn into a jelly bag and leave to drain overnight.

The next day, measure the juice gained and for every 600ml of juice, take 450g warmed sugar. Squeeze the juice from the lemons. Return the apple and berry juice to the pan with the lemon juice and bring gently to the boil. Add the sugar, stirring constantly until it has dissolved, and then bring to the boil again and boil until a set is obtained (see page 36). Pot, seal and label.

Keep overnight before using.

Apple and Plum Chutney

A pleasant, slightly hot chutney – great with any full-flavoured hard cheese and some crusty bread.

MAKES 10 X 375G JARS

1kg green cooking apples

1kg ripe plums

750g red tomatoes

600g onions

2 cucumbers

4 red chillies

1.5 litres malt vinegar

350g brown sugar

75g sea salt

1 teaspoon fresh grated nutmeg

1 teaspoon ground cinnamon

15g mustard seeds

2 small pieces of dried root ginger, bruised

12 black peppercorns

12 whole cloves

small muslin bag for spices

10 x 375g sterilised jam jars (page 44)

Wash, peel and core the apples and chop roughly. Wash, quarter and stone the plums. Wash and chop the tomatoes. Peel and chop the onions. Wash and chop the cucumbers. Chop the chillies, removing the seeds as you go and taking great care not to put your fingers near your eyes or any other tender parts before you have washed them.

Place the vinegar and sugar in a large pan with the salt, nutmeg, cinnamon and mustard seeds. Tie the ginger, peppercorns and cloves into the muslin bag and add this, with the prepared fruit and vegetables, to the pan. Bring gently to the boil and then simmer, stirring occasionally, until the mixture is thick and smooth; this may take up to 2 hours.

Remove the muslin bag. Pot, seal and label.

Keep for at least 1 month before using. Store in a cool, dry place.

End of Season Chutney

A very fruity, mild chutney, which takes advantage of all the last fruits of autumn and will mature well for Christmas. When dealing with a large quantity of fruit, it is perfectly possible to use a food processor, but only use it for a second or two as you do not want to liquidise the ingredients. When buying prunes, don't opt for the most expensive – cheaper ones are fine to use in this chutney.

MAKES 10 X 375G JARS

600g prunes

1kg unripe apples

600g Conference or cooking pears

600g green tomatoes

600g raisins

225g preserved ginger

600g onions

2 large garlic cloves

1 tablespoon sea salt

1 teaspoon cayenne pepper

300ml malt vinegar

1.25kg soft brown sugar

10 x 375g sterilised jam jars (page 44)

Put the prunes in a bowl, cover them with water and leave to soften overnight.

Drain the prunes, remove the stones and whizz the flesh. Peel, core and whizz the apples and pears. Whizz the tomatoes, raisins and ginger. Peel and whizz the onions and garlic.

Put all the ingredients except the vinegar and sugar into a large pan and bring gently to the boil, stirring all the while. Cover and cook without burning, until the mixture is nice and

soft. If it looks in danger of drying out then add a little warm water.

Dissolve the sugar in the vinegar – this prevents the sugar dropping to the bottom of the pan and burning – and add it to the fruity mixture. Bring to the boil stirring constantly and boil gently, uncovered, until thick and smooth. Pot, seal and label.

Keep for 1 month before using.

Fruit Pickle

A wonderful sweet and sour combination of flavours, which is especially good with white meats and soft cheeses. You can use tinned mango – add it after the other fruit has cooked and before adding the sugar. Discard the mango syrup or drink it with soda water.

MAKES 4 X 375G JARS

450g cooking or windfall apples

1 large ripe mango or 240g drained tinned mango

100g stoned dates

50g dried apricots

2 garlic cloves

1 red chilli

1 lemon

1 orange

15g crystallised ginger

150ml white malt vinegar

100g Demerara sugar

250g white granulated sugar

4 x 375g sterilised jam jars (page 44)

Peel, core and cut the apples into small dice. Remove the skin from the fresh mango and cut the fresh or tinned mango flesh into pieces. Chop the dates. Put the apricots in a bowl and cover them with boiling water. Peel and finely chop the garlic. Shred the chilli. Grate the rind and squeeze the juice from the lemon and orange. Roughly chop the ginger. Drain and chop the apricots.

Put all the ingredients, except the sugars and tinned mango, if using, into a pan and cook gently for about 40 minutes until just soft.

Add the tinned mango, if using, and both sugars, stirring well until dissolved, and then bring to a gentle boil. Boil for about 40 minutes until the pickle is thick and translucent, but make sure that it does not burn or become too solid – it will set and thicken on cooling. Pot, seal and label.

Keep for at least 2 weeks before using.

APRICOTS

Apricots are a highly desirable fruit for preserving. Whether fresh, dried or tinned, they make spectacularly beautiful, rich amber goodies reminiscent of hot foreign places and enclosed English gardens. Fresh apricots should be made into luxury preserves, whilst dried apricots are best used in thick, gooey family jams and luscious pickles and chutneys.

Fresh apricots are low in pectin and when buying them for jam making, you should buy the best fruit, ripe, pinky gold, firm and undamaged. To spend effort and money on mediocre fruit is an awful waste of time as the preserve will not set. A straightforward fresh apricot jam will need very little water – approximately 6 tablespoons to the juice of 2 lemons for a weight of 1kg unprepared fruit and 1kg white granulated sugar. Unless you use a commercial pectin or a preserving sugar, the jam will be quite runny and it is for this reason that gooseberries and apples or the juice of either are often used to provide bulk and set to apricot preserves.

Dried apricots are a good buy and the best place to find inexpensive choices is in wholefood shops. The large, more expensive varieties will, with the help of lots of lemon juice, make a good soft jam, whilst the small pieces make excellent economical chutneys and pickles. There is no need to buy the expensive packets of plump, pre-prepared apricots, which are meant for instant consumption. The thing to remember about dried apricots is that they will swell to double their original volume and weight, therefore it is essential to leave them to soak overnight in a large bowl with a good quantity of water – 1.75 litres water should be sufficient to soak 450g dried apricots. This water can also be used to cook the fruit in, but do throw away the unmentionable bits in the bottom of the bowl. This quantity of fruit will need the juice and pips of 3 lemons and approximately 1kg sugar.

FRUIT

Apricot and Gooseberry Jam

A very good jam with an exceptional flavour and, thanks to the gooseberries' high pectin content, an excellent set will be obtained.

MAKES 8 X 375G JARS

1kg fresh, slightly underripe apricots

1kg ripe, green gooseberries

4 large lemons

2kg white granulated sugar

8 x 375g sterilised jam jars (page 44)

Wash, halve and stone the apricots. Wash, top and tail the gooseberries – the easiest way to do this is to snip them off with scissors. Put all the fruit into a large china bowl and squeeze the juice from the lemons over them. Stir in the sugar until all the fruit is covered, place a cloth over the top and leave overnight.

The next day, transfer the contents of the bowl to a preserving pan and bring very gently to the boil, stirring carefully until the sugar has dissolved. Boil rapidly, without burning, until a set is obtained (see page 36). Leave to cool a little, stir once and pot. Seal and label when cold.

This preserve can be eaten the next day or when cold. Store in a cool, dry place.

Apricot and Kumquat Pickle

A really tangy and colourful pickle, which goes well with smoked meats and strong cheese.

MAKES 6 X 375G JARS

500g dried apricots

150g kumquats

1 tablespoon pickling spice

600ml cider vinegar

1 large onion

4 garlic cloves

1 fresh red chilli

1 tablespoon chopped crystallised ginger

500g raisins

2 teaspoons salt

2 teaspoons ground black pepper

250g light brown sugar

1 tablespoon turmeric

6 x 375g sterilised jam jars (page 44)

Wash the apricots, place in a bowl and pour over 1 litre water. Place the kumquats in another bowl and cover them with boiling water.

Leave the apricots and kumquats to soak overnight.

Place the pickling spice and vinegar in a pan and bring to the boil. Remove from the heat, cover and leave overnight.

The next day, drain the apricots in a sieve, retaining 600ml of the water. Drain the kumquats, cut them in half and discard the pips. Place them in a blender and chop until fine. Add the apricots and chop until just broken up.

Peel and finely chop the onion and garlic. Shred the chilli. Place the onion, garlic and chilli in a large pan with the drained apricot water and cook gently until very soft. Add the apricots, kumquats and ginger to the softened onion mixture. Stir well and add the raisins, followed by the strained vinegar, salt and pepper. Cook until very soft, taking care not to burn.

Add the sugar and turmeric and continue to cook over a low heat, stirring constantly until the sugar has dissolved. Keep on a low heat, stirring from time to time until the pickle is thick and well cooked with little excess liquid. Pot, seal and label.

Keep for at least 2 months before using.

Spiced Apricots

Spiced apricots are a deliciously juicy accompaniment to salt meats and spiced sausage. I like to use Hunza apricots for this recipe – they are hard, reddish-brown fruits with the stone still intact. They are not particularly good when eaten as a stewed fruit, but are very receptive to a long immersion in a syrupy liquid.

MAKES 3 X 375G JARS

450g sun-dried Hunza apricots

1 tablespoon whole cloves

1 small cinnamon stick

1 tablespoon whole allspice

900ml white malt vinegar

575g white granulated sugar

small muslin bag for spices

3 x 375g wide-necked sterilised jars (page 44)

Wash the apricots and leave them to soak overnight in a deep bowl of water.

The next day, preheat the oven to 70°C/gas mark ¼.

Tie the spices into the small muslin bag and put them in a preserving pan, add the vinegar and bring to the boil. Add the apricots and simmer until the fruit is just tender, but not broken.

Remove with a slotted spoon, pack into warm, sterilised jars and place in the preheated oven.

Add the sugar to the pan of vinegar and bring gently to the boil, stirring well until the sugar has dissolved. Boil hard until the syrup is thick. Remove the muslin bag and pour the syrup over the apricots to cover them completely and making sure that there are no air bubbles. Seal immediately and label.

Keep for at least 1 month before using.

BANANA

The everyday banana, found in all food shops from the corner grocer to the hypermarket, is relatively cheap to buy, is very high in starch and carbohydrate, easy to eat, a meal in itself and an invaluable, highly nutritive food source. It also forms the basis of some delicious preserves – here are just a couple of my favourites.

Creole Banana Preserve

A sticky, spicy jam with potent, spicy, boozy overtones, so unlike most banana jams it is not really suitable for the nursery! Very good on toasted fruit bread and it makes a delicious fruity toast on a cold winter day. I like to add the rum for a touch of spice, but it is just as nice without.

MAKES 3 X 375G JARS

1kg slightly unripe bananas

675g white granulated sugar or ½ white and ½ soft light brown sugar

1 lime

1 large lemon

½ teaspoon ground cinnamon

½ teaspoon ground allspice

150ml dark rum

3 x 375g sterilised jam jars (page 44)

Peel the bananas and cut them into thick slices, place in a wire basket, metal colander or sieve and dunk briefly in a pan of boiling water. Drain well without breaking.

Put the sugar and 300ml water into a large pan and boil to a thin syrup. Add the banana slices and cook them very gently, not boiling, for approximately 20 minutes.

Peel the lime and the lemon using a potato peeler, ensuring you take no pith, then shred the rind into very fine strips. Blanch the strips for 2 minutes in a pan of boiling water, drain and leave to dry. Squeeze the juice from the lemon and lime and add it to the pan of bananas with the shredded rinds and the spices. Cook gently for 15 minutes until thick.

Remove from the heat, stir in the rum and reboil briefly. Pot, seal and label.

Keep for 1 week before using. Store in a cool, dry place.

Banana Chutney

This is a very tasty chutney, soft and mild and an excellent accompaniment to curry. All the warnings on watching it carefully during cooking really are necessary because this is a thick and volcanic mixture!

MAKES 8 X 375G JARS

1kg bananas

900g apples

450g red tomatoes

2 onions

2 large garlic cloves

1 red chilli

225g block dates (page 137)

25g crystallised ginger

600ml malt vinegar

3 teaspoons salt

1 teaspoon ground allspice

1 teaspoon turmeric

1 teaspoon ground ginger

1 teaspoon ground coriander

350g brown sugar

8 x 375g sterilised jam jars (page 44)

Peel and chop the bananas. Peel, core and chop the apples. Skin and chop the tomatoes (see page 65). Peel and finely chop the onions and garlic. Shred the chilli, deseeding it if you want a milder chutney. Chop the dates and ginger. Put all these ingredients in a large preserving pan with the vinegar, salt and spices. Stir well and cook gently until soft and pulpy. Watch like a hawk to prevent it burning.

Add the sugar, stirring constantly until it has dissolved, and bring gently to the boil. Boil carefully for about 1 hour until thick. Pot, seal and label.

Keep for at least 1 month before using. Store in a cool, dry place.

BLACKBERRY

Blackberries are the most traditional of English fruit and there can be very few of us who have not experienced the pleasure and the pain of picking them. The good housewife of times long past would have considered blackberries to be an essential part of her medicine cabinet as well as a seasonal luxury on her table. The cultivated, and undoubtedly kinder, thornless blackberries are delicious, but lack the unique autumnal taste of the wild ones, better perhaps to keep them for dessert fruit.

Blackberries are low in pectin and it is a good idea to use homemade pectin extract when making jelly or jam. If you have been wise enough to keep a bag of apple cores and peelings in the freezer for just such a contingency, then this is the moment when they can be used, tied into a muslin bag, to stew with your blackberries to give additional set in jelly or jam. If you are prepared to make only small quantities of preserve at a time, then make it with the fruit, lemon juice and sugar, without water. This gives a soft result with the full autumnal flavour of blackberries, which unfortunately will not keep for long, but is delicious nonetheless.

Blackberry and Raspberry Jelly

As these fruits do not come into season together, it will probably be made with the last of the raspberries and the first blackberries of a hot summer. Alternatively, you could use frozen fruit, in which case don't add any water to the pan, but allow them to cook in the liquid in which they defrosted.

MAKES 2 X 375G OR 4 X 175G JARS

500g blackberries

500g raspberries

white granulated or jam sugar, warmed (page 17)

lemons (2 per 500ml juice)

muslin or jelly bag

FRUIT

2 x 375g or 4 x 175g sterilised jam jars
(page 44)

Pick over the fruit, discarding any
mouldy or blemished fruits and
returning any creepy crawlies back to
the garden. Place in a saucepan with
enough water, about 150ml, to prevent
sticking. Cover and simmer until the
fruit is soft, mashing a bit to make
plenty of juice. Turn into a muslin or
jelly bag and leave to drain overnight
into a clean bowl.

The next day, measure the juice
gained and for each 500ml, weigh
out 350g warmed sugar and squeeze
the juice of 2 lemons. Return the fruit
juice to the pan and heat through, add
the lemon juice and sugar and bring
gently to the boil, stirring constantly,
until the sugar has dissolved. Boil hard
until a soft set is obtained (see page
36). Pot, seal and label.

Keep overnight before using.

Potted Blackberries

A really simple-to-make preserve that
keeps very well and has the true taste
of autumn. Eat this chunky preserve
with crackers and light cheeses or
use to boost a good crunchy salad.

MAKES 4 X 375G JARS

1kg blackberries

25g unsalted butter

1kg white granulated or soft light brown
sugar, warmed (page 17)

4 x 375g sterilised jam jars (page 44)

Pick over the blackberries, wash and
shake dry.

Grease a preserving pan with the
butter and put the berries in it over a
low heat. When they become juicy and
start to bubble, pour in the warmed
sugar. Beat hard with a wooden spoon
over a very low heat for 30 minutes,
making sure that the mixture does not
stick or burn, until it is very thick. Pot,
seal and label.

Keep for 2 weeks before using.

Pickled Blackberries

This is the best recipe for pickled blackberries that I have come
across. They are preserved in a light
syrup flavoured with the delicate
scent of geranium. Eat with cold
meats, salamis, cheese and salads.

MAKES 3 X 375G JARS

1kg blackberries

300ml white wine vinegar

450g white granulated sugar

3 rose-scented geranium leaves

3 x 375g sterilised jam jars or pots
(page 44)

Wash and pick over the blackberries. Put the vinegar into a pan with the sugar and heat gently, stirring well until it has dissolved. Add the blackberries and simmer gently for 5 minutes. Do not allow the fruit to become too soft or to break up.

Remove the blackberries from the pan with a slotted spoon and pack into hot, sterilised jars. Keep warm in a low 70°C/gas mark ¼ oven.

Boil the vinegar until it is syrupy. Pop a geranium leaf into each jar and pour the hot syrup over the fruit to cover completely. Seal and label.

Keep for 1 month before using.

Blackberry Cordial

Apart from being a very pleasant cordial, this is an excellent old-fashioned remedy for tummy troubles – 1 small wine glass for adults. Diluted in hot water, it is also a good bedtime drink. You can forego the sterilisation process if you intend to use the cordial within a few days. Dilute to serve with still or sparkling water or it is also very good drunk neat by the small glass after a meal.

MAKES 3 X 500ML BOTTLES

1kg ripe blackberries

450g white granulated sugar

1 teaspoon ground cloves

1 teaspoon ground cinnamon

1 teaspoon grated nutmeg

150ml brandy

muslin cloth for straining

3 x 500ml sterilised bottles with screw caps (page 44)

Pick over the blackberries and briefly rinse under cold water. Place in a saucepan with 500ml water, bring to the boil, reduce the heat, cover and simmer until the fruit has disintegrated. Pass through a fine sieve, making sure that you have all the juice. If there is not enough juice to make up 1 litre, you can add up to 150ml water, but no more.

Boil the blackberry juice and the sugar together, stirring well until it has dissolved. Continue to boil until a syrup has formed. Remove from the heat, skim and add the spices. Stir well, bring to the boil again and continue to simmer for about 20 minutes.

FRUIT

Remove the spiced juice from the heat and allow it to settle, strain through a muslin cloth into a hot metal saucepan. If the juice has become very cool, reheat until it is just at boiling point before pouring into the container. Add the brandy and stir well. Pour the cordial into the sterilised bottles to within 2cm of the tops. Sterilise the filled bottles (see page 44–5)) and label.

Keep for at least 1 week before drinking. Store in the fridge after opening.

FRUIT

BLUEBERRY

The wild blueberry is just too tasty and valuable to use in preserving, but there is rarely a time when cultivated blueberries are unavailable in the shops and there are also many pick-your-own outlets. The fruit is juicy and makes excellent nutritious eating when raw or cooked, savoury or sweet. They make very fine jams and jellies, needing little extra water for good results.

Blueberry and Rhubarb Jelly

A lovely spicy jelly, which goes well with hot croissants and fresh coffee. It also works well with cold meats and cheeses as it is quite sharp.

MAKES 6 X 175G JARS

500g blueberries

500g rhubarb

seeds removed from 1 cardamom pod

1 teaspoon coriander seeds

white granulated sugar, warmed (page 17)

lemons (1 per 600ml juice)

muslin or jelly bag

6 x 175g sterilised jam jars (page 44)

Wash the blueberries. Wash, skin and chop the rhubarb (which should not have been weighed with base or leaves attached, both of which, incidentally, are poisonous).

Crush the spices and place these in a pan with the fruit, add just enough water to prevent sticking (about 150ml), cover tightly and leave to cook very gently, either until the fruit is very flaccid or has made an appreciable amount of juice. You may have to revert to a bit of rough stuff with a wooden spoon in order to break up the berries. Turn the mixture into a clean muslin or jelly bag and leave to drain overnight.

The next day, measure the juice gained and for each 600ml, weigh out 450g warmed sugar and the juice of 1 lemon. Return the juice to the pan and heat gently, add the sugar and lemon juice, stirring constantly until the sugar has dissolved. Bring to the boil and boil hard until a set is obtained (see page 36). Skim, pot, seal and label.

Keep overnight before using.

Blueberry Sauce

A sharp and spicy sauce that is excellent with cold meats and game; particularly good with cold spiced beef.

MAKES 3 X 500ML JARS

1kg blueberries

200ml red wine

6 cloves

6 allspice berries

1 blade mace

1 stick of cinnamon

500g white granulated sugar

small muslin bag for spices

3 x 500ml sterilised Kilner jars (page 44)

Wash the berries and put into a pan with the wine. Tie all the spices in the muslin bag and add to the pan. Bring very gently to the boil, cover and simmer gently for 30 minutes.

Remove the spice bag and put the berries into a liquidiser with 1 cupful of the juices and whizz to form a purée. Pass the purée through a sieve. Return the remainder of the juice to the pan and heat gently, add the purée and sugar, bring gently to the boil, stirring continuously until the sugar is dissolved. Simmer until it is reasonably thick.

Pot and sterilise the filled jars (see page 44–5). This is to be on the safe side for I have found that this sauce can keep well without sterilising.

Keep for at least 2 weeks before using.

FRUIT

CHERRY

I envy anyone who has a cherry tree. Where my sister lives in France great cherry trees flourish abundantly and I wonder why, just across the channel in southern England, we do not have the same bounty. To own a cherry tree is to have glorious pink and white floral displays in the garden in early summer and a good crop of fruit later on, for which the birds will be truly grateful.

There are three different groups of cherries – those suitable for eating raw, those ideal for cooking and preserving and the more versatile varieties that can be enjoyed raw or cooked. White Heart and Napoleon cherries are white through to scarlet and although lovely as a dessert fruit, they will become pale, insipid and flaccid when cooked, lacking any setting qualities at all, and it is generally a waste of time to cook them. May Duke is more versatile and although it's primarily a dessert fruit, it can also be cooked and adapted to preserving.

Dukes, Kentish Reds and Morellos are the best cherries to use for preserving and have the unique distinction of turning any humble jam into a food for the gods. These fruit are deceptive though – they look delectably ripe, juicy and transparent, either glowing red or nearly black, but take a bite and you will be disappointed as they are unhappily tart and acid when eaten raw.

On the whole, although cherries lack good setting properties, they retain both shape and flavour when cooked and produce glorious ruby red and purple preserves. Cherries are sold either as dessert or cooking cherries and, unless you can find a good source, are expensive. Although it may be more sensible, particularly if you have children, to remove the stones from the cherries when making preserves, it is aesthetically more correct to leave them in as they contribute to a better flavour, set and appearance.

FRUIT

Cherry Jam

This is the best jam to make with a mixed bag of cherries, but you should include a fair quantity of cooking cherries for a good flavour.

MAKES 3 X 375G JARS

500g mixed cherries

2 lemons

500g white granulated sugar, warmed (page 17)

125ml commercial pectin

3 x 375g sterilised jam jars (page 44)

Wash the cherries and put them into a pan with 4 tablespoons of water and the juice from the lemons. Cover and cook very gently until the fruit is soft – by which time they should have made more juice.

Remove some of the stones from the fruit, crack them and add them to the pan. Add the warmed sugar, stirring well until it has dissolved, then bring to the boil and boil hard for 3 minutes.

Remove from the heat and stir in the pectin. Return to the heat and as soon as the jam threatens to rise out of the pan whip it off immediately. Skim, removing any stray stones that may have risen to the top. Allow to cool before potting, giving an occasional stir to distribute the fruit. Pot and label. Seal when cold.

Keep overnight before using.

Summer Preserve

The best of summer fruit go into this preserve and if you make it properly, you will have a confection similar to summer pudding to spread on bread and toast throughout the winter.

MAKES 4 X 375G JARS

500g Mayduke or Morello cherries

350g raspberries

350g mixed red and white currants

1 lemon

750g white granulated sugar, warmed (page 17)

4 x 375g sterilised jam jars (page 44)

Wash the cherries. Wash and hull the raspberries. Wash and string the currants. Squeeze the juice from the lemon. Put the cherries in a pan with 2 tablespoons of water and the lemon juice and cook very gently, watching like a hawk to prevent burning. If the fruit does dry out before the cherries have made enough juice, then add a very little more water. When there is a fair amount of juice, cover and simmer for 10 minutes.

Add the raspberries and currants and cook uncovered, over a moderate heat, stirring occasionally until all the fruit is just soft. Bring to the boil and boil for 5 minutes. Add the warmed sugar, stirring constantly until it has dissolved, and then boil until a set is achieved (see page 36). Pot, seal and label.

Keep overnight before using.

Brandied Cherries

The syrupy alcohol is delicious in drinks. Use a small amount in a cooling summer drink of champagne or white wine, as in a Kir, or the abstemious might prefer it with soda or sparkling water. The cherries make superb grown-up desserts.

MAKES 1 X 750G JAR

500g cooking cherries, preferably Morello or another dark variety

300g caster sugar

300ml brandy

1 x 750g sterilised Kilner or bottling jar (page 44)

Wash and pat dry the cherries – you can use them with or without a small piece of stalk. Put them into the jar and, as you place each layer, sprinkle with a good cushion of sugar. Continue in this way until all the cherries and sugar are used up.

Fill the jar up with brandy, making sure that all the fruit is covered. Tilt the jar to ensure that there are no air bubbles. Seal tightly and label. Put in a cool, dark place for at least 1 week, turning the jar over and back each day. Then, leave the fruit to happily macerate and for the brandy to settle. Do not be tempted to open for at least 1 month!

CRANBERRY

I was first introduced to cranberries many years ago by a Polish friend of mine and I thought then that it seemed extraordinary that Europe, which gave birth to the cranberry, no longer gives it more than a passing glance. Nowadays we all know of the health benefits of cranberry juice, but few people know of its other merits. Although the cranberry is tart and nasty to eat raw, and has variable pectin content, it does make the most delicious fillings for pies and pastries and excellent sharp preserves, which have a completely unique flavour.

Cranberries come to this country from America, where they have an historical connection with Thanksgiving. Fresh cranberries are in season in the autumn, but frozen berries can be used at other times of the year. If you do use frozen cranberries, allow them to gently defrost and use the juice to add to the liquid you cook them in.

Cranberry Marmalade

The cranberries disintegrate in this special marmalade to give it a lovely, glorious glowing translucence and a unique flavour. This makes a special festive breakfast preserve.

MAKES 3 X 375G JARS

500g cranberries

1½ grapefruits

6 oranges

350g raisins

75g walnuts

1.4kg white granulated sugar, warmed (page 17)

3 x 375g sterilised jam jars (page 44)

Wash the cranberries. Wash the grapefruit and oranges, peel the skin off in strips and roughly chop the fruit, discarding the pith. Then, either finely chop or use a blender to process the fruit pulp and peel.

Put all the fruit, their juices and the raisins into a pan with 900ml water and bring gently to the boil, stirring well to avoid sticking. Cover and cook for about 40 minutes until very soft. Transfer to a china bowl, cover and leave overnight. This will allow the peels to soften further.

The next day, transfer the fruit back

to the pan and bring to the boil. Chop the walnuts and add to the pan with the warmed sugar. Bring gently to the boil, stirring constantly until the sugar has dissolved. Boil rapidly until a set is obtained (see page 36). Pot, seal and label.

Keep for at least 2 weeks before using.

Cranberry Chutney

This is a wonderfully sweet and tangy chutney to serve with slices of cold turkey on Boxing Day.

MAKES 3 X 375G JARS

2 onions

2 large garlic cloves

600ml white malt vinegar

500g cranberries

250g hard eating or cooking apples

250g pitted prunes

1 large orange

1 small red chilli

1 teaspoon sea salt

250g white granulated or soft brown sugar

1 tablespoon mixed peel

3 x 375g sterilised jam jars (page 44)

Peel and chop the onions and garlic. Place them in a small pan with 150ml of the vinegar. Cook until soft.

Wash the cranberries. Peel, core and chop the apples. Chop the prunes. Grate the rind from the orange and squeeze the juice. Shred the chilli. Put all these ingredients into a large pan with the salt and the onion, garlic and vinegar mixture, cook gently until soft.

Stir in the sugar until it has dissolved and add the chopped peel. Bring to the boil and boil until thick. Pot, seal and label.

Keep for 1 month before using.

Cranberry and Kumquat Pickle

A somewhat astringent pickle, which is very good with cold game, turkey, pâtés and terrines. The Lexia raisins have a very rich, distinctive flavour.

MAKES 4 X 375G JARS

1 large onion

1 garlic clove

700g cranberries

250g kumquats

150g Lexia raisins

¼ teaspoon ground cinnamon

¼ teaspoon ground allspice

½ teaspoon dried chilli flakes

300ml white malt vinegar

450g white granulated sugar

4 x 375g sterilised jam jars (page 44)

Peel and finely chop the onion and garlic and put them in a pan with the cranberries. Add just enough water to cover and cook until soft.

Halve and finely chop the kumquats and cook these separately in a very small amount of water, making sure that you discard the pips as you go. When they are soft, add the kumquats to the cranberry mixture. Roughly chop the raisins and add to the pan with the spices, chilli and vinegar and cook until the liquid is much reduced and the mixture is very thick.

Add the sugar, stirring well until it has dissolved, bring to the boil and

continue to cook, stirring occasionally, until soft and thick. Pot, seal and label. Keep for 1 month before using.

CURRANTS

The currants referred to on the next few pages are the members of the Ribes family, which are edible, that is the blackcurrant, redcurrant and white currant, not to be confused with the black and shrivelled little object that is the dried Corinth grape used in cake making. The jams, preserves, pickles and beverages that may be made from these currants are amongst the very best to be offered in the culinary world; some are strong and rich and full of sharp flavour, others delicate and subtle. Not only do they taste good, but they have the most glorious appearance, are full of vitamins, give a good yield per kilogram and always set remarkably well. What more could one ask of any fruit?

Blackcurrant and Rum Preserve

A deliciously mellow preserve, which spreads well and retains the whole fruit and which chaps are very fond of. For a basic, but nonetheless nice jam, simply leave out the rum.

MAKES 3 X 375G JARS

500g blackcurrants

750g white granulated sugar, warmed (page 17)

4 tablespoons rum

3 x 375g sterilised jam jars (page 44)

Remove the currants from the stalk using the tines of a fork, wash and place in a pan (do take care not to use copper as the high acid content in the currants reacts unfavourably with it), Add 450ml water and bring to the boil, reduce the heat and simmer gently, stirring occasionally, until the skins are very soft, testing with the odd nibble to make sure.

When the fruit is cooked and the contents of the pan reduced by half, add the warmed sugar and heat gently, stirring well until it has dissolved. Bring to the boil and boil hard until a set is obtained (see page 36). Add the rum and stir well. Skim, pot, seal and label. Keep for 2 weeks before using.

Blackcurrant and Apple Jelly Jam

Unless you have a good source of pick-your-own fruit, blackcurrants can be quite expensive. This recipe has the double advantage of being economical and children will appreciate the milder flavour and the lack of pips.

MAKES 5 X 375G JARS

500g blackcurrants

500g cooking apples

white granulated sugar, warmed (page 17)

5 x 375g sterilised jam jars (page 44)

Remove the currants from the stalks using the tines of a fork and wash them well. Peel and core the apples and place both fruits into a pan with 600ml water. Cook gently until all the fruit is soft.

Pass the cooked fruit through a fine sieve, leaving only the pips behind. Weigh the pulp gained and for each 500g, take 500g warmed sugar. Return the purée to the pan and heat through, taking care not to burn. Add the sugar, stirring well, until it has dissolved, then bring to the boil and boil hard until a set is obtained (see page 36). Pot, seal and label.

Keep for 2 weeks before using.

Blackcurrant Shrub

This is a very old-fashioned word from the Arabic *shurb* or *shuriba* – to drink – also from sherbet, another Arabic drink. Drink it either as an after-dinner noggin or in hot water for colds and coughs, etc.

MAKES 2 X 500ML BOTTLES

500g blackcurrants

Demerara sugar

1 x 750ml bottle of dark rum

muslin or jelly bag

filter paper

1 x 1 litre sterilised jar and 2 x 500ml sterilised bottles with corks (page 44)

Remove the currants from the stalks using the tines of a fork and wash them well. Place them in a pan with just enough water to prevent them from sticking. Bring to the boil, cover and reduce the heat to simmering. Cook until the fruit is totally soft and has yielded

up all its juices. Turn into a muslin or jelly bag and leave to drain completely overnight into a clean china bowl.

Measure out the resulting liquid and for every 600ml juice, weigh out 450g sugar. Place the juice and sugar in the jar with 375ml rum per 600ml juice. Seal, shake well and leave in a cool place for 1 week, stirring and shaking 4 times a day.

Strain through a filter paper, pour into sterilised bottles and cork securely.

Keep for 1 month before using.

Redcurrant Jelly

Whilst the basic recipe is delicious, there are lots of ways to make this a little bit special. A dessertspoon of pickling spice can be bruised and added to the currants whilst they are cooking and this will give a more aromatic jelly. Juniper berries crushed and added to the cooking fruit gives a good astringent jelly, whilst chopped fresh or dried thyme added either to the pan of cooking fruit or just prior to potting will make a jelly that is authentically rural and is splendid with game or for adding to gravy.

MAKES 6 X 175G JARS

500g redcurrants
white granulated sugar, warmed (page 17)
muslin or jelly bag
6 x 175g sterilised jam jars (page 44)

Remove the currants from the stalks using the tines of a fork, wash them well. Put them in a large pan with 450ml water. Bring to the boil and cook gently for 15 minutes, resorting to a bit of bashing with a wooden spoon to ensure that the fruit is well broken up. Pour into a muslin or jelly bag and leave to drip overnight into a china bowl, do not be tempted to prod or squeeze – this will spoil the clear appearance.

The next day, measure the juice and for each 600ml, weigh out 450g warmed sugar. Return the juice to the pan and bring it gently to the boil. Add the sugar, stirring well until it has dissolved and bring to the boil. Boil until a set is obtained (see page 36). Skim, pot, seal and label.

Keep overnight before using.

Redcurrant Conserve

A lovely combination of flavours, which works equally well on toast as it does with cheese. If you prefer the orange skins to be softer, then process the slices in a blender, but do remove the pips first.

MAKES 3 X 375G JARS

500g redcurrants
1 large, thin-skinned sweet orange
150g Lexia raisins
500g white granulated sugar, warmed (page 17)
3 x 375g sterilised jam jars (page 44)

Remove the currants from the stalks using the tines of a fork and wash them well. Working on a plate to catch the juices, thinly slice the orange, removing the pips. Chop the raisins.

Put all the fruit and collected juices into a pan. Warm through until the juices begin to run and when the fruit starts to simmer, add the warmed sugar and stir constantly to prevent sticking. Bring gently to the boil, stirring well until the sugar has dissolved. Boil for 20 minutes, when a set should be obtained (see page 36). Pot, seal and label.

This can be eaten the next day or when cold. Store in a cool, dry place.

Remove the currants from the stalks using the tines of a fork and wash them well.

Put all the remaining ingredients into a pan and bring gently to the boil, stirring continuously to ensure that the sugar has dissolved. Boil rapidly for a further 5 minutes, add the currants and simmer until they are quite tender. Leave to cool a little and stir well before potting. Seal and label when cold.

Keep for 1 week before using.

Spiced Redcurrant Relish

A useful recipe and a pleasant relish. A good companion to game, venison, mutton and cold Christmas turkey.

MAKES 2 X 375G JARS

500g redcurrants

375g soft light brown sugar

300ml cider vinegar

1 dessertspoon ground allspice

1 dessertspoon ground cloves

1 dessertspoon fresh grated nutmeg

1 dessertspoon ground cinnamon

1 teaspoon sea salt

2 x 375g sterilised jam jars (page 44)

 A type of plum originally from Damascus (hence the name), but now rarely seen in our shops. Like so many traditional British fruit, the damson is nutritious, tasty and economical and, being very high in pectin, is the home-preserver's friend. In fact the sharp, rich jams, pickles and cheeses that are made with damsons are some of the great classical country recipes of Britain, but it is a fruit that is fast disappearing.

A good hint for removing stones from hard plums, damsons,

sloe or bullace (wild plums), etc, is to stir in a knob of unsalted butter after the sugar has been added, and then they should slide merrily to the surface.

Damson and Port Preserve

A pleasant rich preserve, especially good on wholemeal toast.

MAKES 2 X 375G JARS

500g damsons

1 lemon

150ml light port wine

750g white granulated sugar, warmed (page 17)

small muslin bag

2 x 375g sterilised jam jars (page 44)

Wash the damsons and prick them with a needle to encourage the juices to flow. Squeeze the juice and remove the pips from the lemon and reserve both. Tie the pips into the small muslin bag. Place the bag, damsons and port in a china bowl, cover and leave overnight, turning from time to time.

The next day, pop the damson and port mixture into a preserving pan with 150ml water and the lemon juice. Bring to the boil and then simmer carefully until the fruit is soft without becoming mushy. Remove any stones that rise to the top, endeavouring to crack a few and reserve the kernels. Remove the muslin bag and add the warmed sugar to the pan, heat gently and stir well until the sugar is dissolved. Bring to the boil and boil until a set is obtained (see page 36). Remove from the heat and stir in the kernels, fishing out any floating stones before you pot. Seal and label. Keep for 1 week before using.

Damson Cheese

Cheeses and butters have a much denser consistency and a more intense flavour than jams. Cheeses particularly can be kept a considerable time. They should be turned out of their pots, sliced and served with after-dinner cheese and biscuits or with a good crisp salad. Although a little crusty to look at, this cheese is sharp with a pleasant almondy flavour. Sloe, bullacé and small blue plums also make excellent cheeses using the same recipe. Try an excellent gooseberry cheese or experiment with blackcurrant and

black cherry with a dash of rum.
Quince or apple and plum also work
well – the choices for making fruit
cheeses are extensive, in fact as far
as your imagination takes you, but
the method is the same. Butters are
made in the same way, but are not
cooked for so long in order that they
stay spreadable rather than sliceable.

1kg damsons
white granulated sugar, warmed
(page 17)
Sunflower oil or other flavourless oil,
for oiling
100–125ml sterilised moulds (page 44)
greaseproof paper and rubber bands
or string

Wash the damsons and put them into
an ovenproof earthenware or china
dish with 1 tablespoon of water. Cover
and leave in the oven overnight.

The next day, when the juices have
run and the damsons are soft, pass
them through a fine sieve. Crack some
of the stones and remove the kernels,
chop them and add them to the purée
(they give a nice nutty flavour to the
preserve).

Weigh the pulp and for every 500g
gained, weigh out 500g warmed
sugar. Place the fruit pulp and sugar
|in a clean pan and heat gently,
stirring well until the sugar has
dissolved. Bring to the boil and boil
until the cheese is very thick and
leaves the sides of the pan with no
surplus moisture.

Brush the moulds with a very fine
film of the oil.

Divide the cheese among the moulds
and cover with a double folding of
greaseproof paper, tied down with a
rubber band or string. Label.

Keep for at least 2 months before
using.

DATE

The first tree that any of us draw. Until relatively recently, few of us would have recognised the fruit as it grows on the tree, surrounded by a thick green or red outer skin and bearing no resemblance to the soft, sticky fruit that we buy in Britain. Although there are many different varieties of dates on the market, from the expensive Medjool date and the semi-dried dates in boxes, which are popular at Christmas, the most useful for the cook are the dried, compressed dates bought in economical blocks. Dates are sweet, sticky and nutritious and make really excellent preserves and chutneys, for not only do they give a good, thick, rich texture, but the amount of sugar usually necessary in the recipe is often much reduced.

Date and Apricot Spread

A very yummy preserve, with Middle Eastern overtones and one that is very useful to make in winter when all else eludes you. Children love it.

MAKES 4 X 375G JARS

50g blanched almonds

275g dried apricots

500g block dates

1 lemon

225g soft light brown or white granulated sugar, warmed (page 17)

4 x 375g sterilised jam jars (page 44)

Chop the almonds into small pieces and gently toast them, either by placing on a metal tray under the grill or by putting them in a hot oven and leaving for 5 minutes, though in both cases watch like a hawk to prevent burning. Put the apricots into a deep bowl, cover with 1 litre water and leave to soak overnight.

The next day, put the apricots and the water they were soaked in (apart from the gritty bits at the bottom) into a pan. Chop the dates, add these to the pan and cook until very soft.

Squeeze the juice from the lemon. Add the warmed sugar and the lemon juice, heat gently, stirring well until the sugar has dissolved. Bring to a gentle boil and simmer, stirring very frequently, until the spread is thick. Add the toasted almonds, stirring them into the mixture, and cook for a few more minutes. Pot, seal and label.

Keep for 2 weeks before using. Store in a cool, dry place.

Date and Lemon Chutney

Very tasty with ham or any highly spiced food. Hot as hell and sweet as sin – enjoy!

MAKES 3 X 375G JARS

500g block dates

4 medium-sized onions

2 large garlic cloves

3 thin-skinned lemons

1 small fresh red chilli

600ml malt vinegar

125g soft brown sugar

2 tablespoons black treacle

1 dessertspoon sea salt

125g sultanas

3 x 375g sterilised jam jars (page 44)

Chop the dates. Peel and finely chop the onions and garlic. Grate the rind from 2 of the lemons and take the flesh and juice from all 3. Shred the chilli.

Put the vinegar in a pan with the sugar, treacle and salt and bring to the boil. Simmer for 5 minutes, making sure that the sugar is dissolved, then add all the other ingredients and bring gently to the boil. Reduce the heat and simmer until very soft; about 45 minutes. Pot, seal and label.

Keep for 1 month before using.

FRUIT

ELDERBERRY

The elderberry is one of the most prolific and abundant trees that grow in the British Isles. In the spring it carries the most beautiful mass of frothy, white, sweet-scented flowers, which more than any other flower have lent themselves to magic cures and modern cosmetics.

Elderflowers when used in preserves impart an extraordinary Muscatel flavour to even the most mundane fruit. A small bunch picked before the sun reaches its zenith, tied without stalks into a muslin bag and popped into any preserve, will raise it to the luxury class.

Elderberries, small and purple-black, grow in umbrella-like clusters that, when ripe, turn upside down. The taste, when raw, is sharp yet sickly, but they blend very well with other hedgerow fruit to make good preserves and interesting sauces. Pick the fruit on a dry day and weigh it off the stem.

September Jam

A deliciously sharp, autumnal jam. Hedgerow jams can be given a real fillip if you use the left-over fruit from your Sloe Gin (page 213), Blackberry Cordial (pages 121–2), Blackcurrant Shrub (page 132) or Raspberry Ratafia (page 208).

MAKES 6 X 375G JARS

500g elderberries

500g blackberries

500g cooking apples

250g damsons or sloes

1.75g white granulated sugar, warmed (page 17)

6 x 375g sterilised jam jars (page 44)

Wash and strip the elderberries from the stalk using the tines of a fork, discarding any nasty bits – particularly look out for any rogue blackfly! Put them in a pan with 250ml water and cook gently until they are very soft.

Wash the blackberries and leave to dry on kitchen paper. Peel, core and quarter the apples. Prick the damsons or sloes with a needle. Put these fruit into a large pan and strain the juice from the elderberries over them. Bring to the boil and cook gently, stirring occasionally until the fruit is soft and the juice has reduced slightly. Add the warmed sugar and stir well until it has dissolved. Bring to the boil and boil rapidly until a set is reached (see page 36). Remove any stones that may have risen to the top. Skim, pot, seal and label.

Keep for 1 week before using.

Pontacks Sauce

A sauce made with elderberries that goes back to medieval days, but Pontac, or Pontacks, sauce became a commercial sauce in the late 1800s when anchovies were added. Use up to 1 tablespoon to spice up meat dishes, especially shepherd's pie.

MAKES 4 X 175ML BOTTLES

500g elderberries

1 tablespoon black peppercorns

600ml robust red wine or red wine vinegar or 300ml red wine and 300ml red wine vinegar

125g shallots

1 teaspoon cloves

1 blade mace

1 large piece of dried root ginger, bruised

1 teaspoon sea salt

4 x 175ml sterilised bottles with corks (page 44)

Preheat the oven to 70°C/gas mark ¼. Wash and strip the elderberries from the stalk using the tines of a fork, discarding any nasty bits. Put the fruit into an earthenware casserole with the peppercorns. Place the wine or vinegar in a small pan and bring it to the boil, pour it over the elderberries, cover with a lid and place in the oven overnight.

The next day, peel and finely chop the shallots and put them with the remaining spices and salt into a pan (do not use an enamelled pan, you will never get the stain out!). Add the strained juice from the elderberries and bring to the boil. Boil gently for about 10 minutes.

Remove from the heat, cover and allow to cool.

Strain carefully, return the sauce to a clean pan and return to the boil just once more. Bottle, seal and label.

Keep for 1 month before using.

FIG

FIG Anyone who has sampled the delights of the sweet, odoriferous flesh of a fresh ripe fig picked from a Mediterranean hillside will consider packing up and leaving these isles for that pleasure alone and will probably consider that it is a philistine thing to preserve them in any way at all. However, in Britain most figs do not reach the luscious and decadent maturity of brown or green figs grown in southern Europe, although a surplus of underripe fruit may be made good use of. Dried figs bear little resemblance to the fresh fruit and they come in many guises, from the elegant and expensive whole fruit to the tiny dried figs that make wonderful spiced and pickled fruit, but the most economical are those sold in solid blocks, which can be used to great advantage in marvellous winter jams and chutneys.

Fresh Fig Preserve with Sherry

Very pleasant and lovely and boozy – excellent on ice cream. It is best to use figs that are just becoming soft, denoting that they are thinking about ripening.

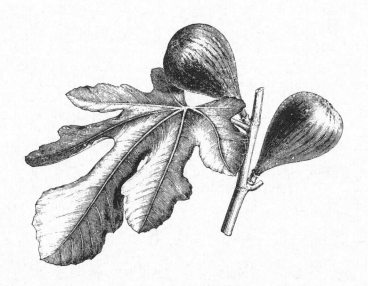

MAKES 2 X 375G JARS

500g fresh figs

1 lemon

1 orange

500g white granulated sugar, warmed
(page 17)

4 tablespoons sweet sherry

2 x 375g sterilised jam jars (page 44)

Put the figs into a large china bowl and cover them completely with boiling water. Leave to soak for 5 minutes. Drain, pat dry and chop into small pieces, removing any hard tail ends.

Place the figs in a pan with the zest and juice from the lemon and the orange and heat through. Bring to the

boil and cook on a low heat until the fruit is tender, taking care not to burn it. Add the warmed sugar and heat gently, stirring well until it has dissolved.

Bring to the boil and simmer, stirring occasionally, until a clear syrup forms. Bring to the boil, add the sherry, stir well and leave to become cool before potting. Seal and label when cold.

Keep for 2 weeks before using.

Pickled Baby Figs

Many wholefood shops keep these little figs, and as they are quite hard, they take very well to being bathed in a rich syrup and are quite

deliciously unusual. An asset for the cold table, they go with pâtés, terrines and cold meats.

MAKES 2 X 375G JARS

500g small, whole dried figs

500g soft light brown sugar

300ml cider vinegar

1 tablespoon ground aniseed

1 tablespoon ground mace

1 tablespoon ground cinnamon

1 tablespoon ground allspice

2 x 375g sterilised jam jars with wide necks (page 44)

Wash the figs, place them in a large bowl and cover well with cold water to allow for the fruit expanding. Leave overnight.

The next day, drain the figs and pat dry. Put the sugar, vinegar and spices into a large pan and bring to the boil, stirring well until the sugar has dissolved. Continue to boil until a thin syrup has formed. Add the figs and simmer gently until the fruit is soft without breaking up and the syrup is thick. Pot, seal and label.

Keep for 1 month before using.

Glencar Jam

I believe that the Glencar was an hotel in Westmorland, which prided itself on its innovative home cooking. A very tasty, bright clear jam, which improves on keeping.

MAKES 3 X 375G JARS

500g rhubarb stems

225g block figs

100g candied lemon or citron peel

1 small lemon

500g white granulated sugar

3 x 375g sterilised jam jars (page 44)

Wash, trim or string the rhubarb and cut it into pieces. Chop the figs very small. Finely chop the candied lemon peel. Squeeze the juice from the lemon and put all the ingredients into a china bowl. Cover and leave to stand for 24 hours.

Transfer the mixture to a pan and heat gently, stirring well, until all the sugar has dissolved. Bring to the boil and boil hard until a set is obtained (see page 36). Pot, seal and label.

Keep for 1 month before using.

GOOSEBERRY

One of the great disappointments of my young life was to find that very little grew under the gooseberry bushes in our garden except well-composted earth! Another was that after pricking my fingers mercilessly on the thorns, the prized reward of a juicy-looking red berry did not live up to expectations and shrivelled my mouth with its sharpness.

If you are fortunate enough to grow your own fruit bushes, then you will know that the best varieties to grow are those that crop heavily early in the year and may be picked whilst relatively unripe and used for preserving, leaving a substantial quantity on the bush to swell and ripen to give prime dessert fruit. Keepsake is a good example, whilst Lancashire Lad and Careless mature later and are excellent for cooking and preserving. Levellers should be kept as a dessert fruit as they are utterly delicious. Gooseberries make marvellous preserves as they are full of flavour and have a high pectin content, giving few problems. Make gooseberry pectin extract as for apple pectin extract.

Soft Gooseberry Jelly Jam

A good, fresh and spreadable jam with no pips or skin, therefore ideal for small children and those senior adults whose teeth are not as good as they might be. The double trouble of both crushing, then sieving, ensures that you have all the goodness of the fruit without the addition of water. When making gooseberry jam I like to trail a bunch of elderflowers through the cooking preserve as in Elderflower Jelly (see page 45) – this gives a subtle floral flavour to the finished jam.

MAKES 2 X 375G JARS

500g gooseberries

white granulated sugar, warmed (page 17)

1 lemon

½ teaspoon vanilla extract

2 x 375g sterilised jam jars (page 44)

FRUIT

Wash the gooseberries and crush them with a blunt object or put them through a blender. Turn the resulting purée into a pan, boil for 5 minutes and then pass through a fine sieve. Weigh the pulp gained and for each 500g gained, weigh out 500g warmed sugar. Squeeze the juice from the lemon.

Return the pulp, sugar and lemon juice to the clean pan and heat gently, stirring well until the sugar has dissolved. Bring to the boil and boil for approximately 15 minutes, stirring frequently and taking great care not to burn. Stir in the vanilla extract. Pot, seal and label.

Keep overnight before using.

Gooseberry and Loganberry Jam

Loganberries are similar to large raspberries, but slightly sharper. Gooseberry and raspberry or goose-berry and blackberry jam can also be made using this recipe. A soft pip-free jam can be made using the same ingredients as below, but following the method given for Soft Gooseberry Jelly Jam (above).

MAKES 5 X 375G JARS

500g red gooseberries

500g firm loganberries

1kg white granulated sugar, warmed (page 17)

5 x 375g sterilised jam jars (page 44)

Wash, top and tail the gooseberries. Leave the loganberries to soak in lightly salted water for 30 minutes to get rid of deeply embedded small wriggly things.

Place the gooseberries in a pan with just enough water, about 150ml, to prevent them sticking and simmer gently until just soft. Drain the loganberries well, they should now be quite free of any wildlife, and add them to the pan. Cook for 10 minutes, by which time both fruits should be soft.

Add the warmed sugar and stir carefully until it has dissolved. Bring to the boil and boil hard until a set is obtained (see page 36). Pot, seal and label.

Keep for 1 month before using.

Cassandra's Gooseberry Conserve

Cassandra was a very batty artist friend who used the same verve and imagination in her cooking as she did in her painting. A rich and tasty conserve with just a hint of fruity booziness.

MAKES 4 X 375G JARS

100g dried apricots

100g dried figs

125ml sweet sherry

500g red gooseberries

450g white granulated sugar, warmed (page 17)

4 x 375g sterilised jam jars (page 44)

Wash the dried fruits well and finely chop them, put them in a bowl with the sherry. Cover and leave overnight.

The next day, wash, top and tail the gooseberries and place them in a pan with 600ml water, bring gently to the boil and then simmer until the fruit is just soft and the liquid reduced.

Stir in the dried fruit, which should have expanded nicely in the sherry, and cook until the fruit is soft and well mixed. Add the warmed sugar, stirring

well until it has dissolved and continue to boil until a set is obtained (see page 36). Pot, seal and label.

Keep overnight before using.

Elderflower Jelly

A splendid delicate jelly, heady with the elegant, flowery Muscatel perfume of elderflower. If you pick the flower heads too early, they will have become stale by the time that they are used. However, you can put them into a plastic bag and pop them in the freezer until gooseberries come into season. Lovely in a Victoria sponge sandwich or on homemade biscuits and with bread and butter.

MAKES 8 X 175G JARS

1kg gooseberries

white granulated sugar, warmed (page 17)

6 large fresh elderflower heads, picked after the juice has drained

muslin or jelly bag

8 x 175g sterilised jam jars (page 44)

Wash the gooseberries and put them into a pan with 300ml water. Simmer until very soft, mashing if necessary. Turn into a muslin or jelly bag and leave to drain overnight into a clean bowl.

The next day, measure the juice and for each 600ml gained, weigh out 450g warmed sugar.

Clean the elderflowers by shaking them upside down and examining them microscopically for any livestock. Do not wash them if you can possibly help it for they will lose much of their magic perfume.

Place the juice in a pan and heat gently, add the sugar, stirring well until it has dissolved. Bring to the boil and while you are boiling to a set, drift and twirl the elderflowers across the jelly, holding them by their stems. Do not worry about a few petals becoming transfixed in the jelly, they will look absolutely delightful. When a set is obtained (see page 36), skim, pot, seal and label.

Keep overnight before using.

Gooseberry Chutney

A mild, fruity chutney that makes a particularly good accompaniment to light salty cheeses such as Caerphilly.

MAKES 3 X 375G JARS

500g gooseberries

100g sultanas

2 medium-sized onions

150g soft brown sugar

1 teaspoon ground mixed spice

1 teaspoon mustard powder

1 tablespoon sea salt

225ml malt vinegar

3 x 375g sterilised jam jars (page 44)

Wash, top and tail the gooseberries. Chop the sultanas. Peel and chop the onions and put them in a small pan with just enough water to cover. Cook the onions until just soft and then drain.

Put the drained onions with the gooseberries and all the other ingredients into a pan and heat gently, stirring well. Bring to the boil and then simmer until thick, stirring frequently to prevent burning. Pot, seal and label.

Keep for 1 month before using.

Gooseberry and Garlic Pickle

A hot and extremely pungent pickle, also known fondly as Death Breath! Especially good with cold meats, a cold meat pie and robust cheeses.

MAKES 2 X 375G JARS

500g unripe or hard green gooseberries

125g soft light brown sugar

400ml white malt vinegar

150g raisins

1 dessertspoon ground black pepper

100g mustard seeds (a mixture of black, yellow and brown is good)

100g peeled garlic cloves

1 teaspoon cayenne pepper

1 teaspoon sea salt

2 x 375g sterilised jam jars (page 44)

Wash, top and tail the gooseberries and put into a pan with the sugar and half the vinegar. Heat gently, stirring well until the sugar has dissolved. Bring to the boil and then simmer for about 40 minutes until the fruit is soft.

Chop the raisins. Grind or pound the black pepper, mustard seeds, peeled garlic and cayenne together with the salt (the rough salt acts as a grinding agent) in a bowl and add this, with the raisins, to the pan. Stir in the remaining vinegar, bring to the boil and boil hard for 5 minutes, stirring well. Pot, seal and label.

Keep for at least 3 months before using. Store in a cool, dry place

Spiced Gooseberry Pickle

This is a truly delicious combination of flavours, which are outstanding with cold meats and cheese. The same recipe also works awfully well with tinned gooseberries – use the gooseberry juice instead of water and reduce the sugar by 2 tablespoonfuls. Tinned gooseberries will only need to be heated through before adding the remainder of the ingredients.

MAKES 3 X 375G JARS

500g gooseberries

1 thin-skinned sweet orange

1 thin-skinned lemon

125g sultanas

a large piece of dried root ginger

1 cinnamon stick

1 blade mace

1 dessertspoon cloves

625g soft light brown sugar

300ml red wine vinegar

small muslin bag for spices

3 x 375g sterilised jam jars (page 44)

Wash, top and tail the gooseberries and put them in a pan with 100ml water. Cook until the skins are tender.

Wash and thinly slice the orange and lemon, removing the pips and saving the juice. Although I prefer the thin slices, you can mince or put the fruit through a food processor for a very brief whizz, but do remember to remove the pips. Wash

FRUIT

the sultanas. Bruise the spices and tie them into the small muslin bag.

Put all the ingredients into the pan with the gooseberries. Heat gently, stirring well until the sugar has dissolved. Bring to the boil and simmer, stirring frequently, for about 1 hour until the mixture is thick. Remove the muslin bag. Pot, seal and label.

Keep for at least 3 months before using. Store in a cool, dry place.

Gooseberry and Elderflower Syrup

This syrup has the fragrance of Muscatel, as anyone who has ever made elderflower wine will know. Dilute with water or soda for a cooling summer drink. Do not throw the gooseberries away – sieve them for making a gooseberry fool by taking 500ml of the sieved gooseberries and stirring in 225g caster sugar (unless the fruit was cooked with sugar). Whip in 400ml double cream and leave to get very cold. If economy dictates, you can use 200ml double cream and 200ml thick custard.

MAKES 4 X 500ML OR 2 X 1 LITRE BOTTLES

1kg green gooseberries

1kg white granulated sugar

3 large fresh elderflower heads, picked after the juice has drained

string

muslin cloth for straining

4 x 500ml or 2 x 1 litre sterilised bottles (page 44)

Wash the gooseberries. Put the sugar and 750ml water into a large pan and bring slowly to boiling point, stirring well. As soon as a syrup is formed, add the gooseberries and simmer until the skins are soft.

Clean the elderflower heads by turning them upside down and shaking well. Tie the stems together with the string. As the syrup is beginning to boil, plunge the heads in, holding the string to keep the stems above the syrup, bring rapidly to the boil and remove the pan from the heat. Strain through the muslin, bottle and label.

The syrup may be sterilised in the bottles (see pages 44–5), but this is not really necessary unless you wish to keep it for more than a month, but as it is so delicious this rarely happens.

Let settle for 24 hours before using.

GRAPES

Grapes have become so much a part of our lives nowadays that no one would consider raising an outraged shriek at the thought of using them to make elegant preserves. Grapes left over at the end of the season and that have not matured well will make good preserves. The most expensive black grapes should be kept for preserves that require that the fruit is kept whole or for steeping in brandy. Most shop-bought grapes make interesting and different preserves, although it should be remembered that grapes have absolutely no pectin content. Fortunately, recipes using gooseberry, crab apple and currant juice can be easily adapted to preserve small, sweet green grapes.

Grape Conserve

An unusual and deliciously expensive preserve for your friends. A good-quality, pure and natural grape juice can be used instead of making your own – use just enough to cover the fruit in the pan.

MAKES 6 X 375G JARS

1kg black grapes

500g Conference or cooking pears

500g cooking apples

1kg white granulated sugar

6 x 375g sterilised jam jars (page 44)

Squeeze the grapes, either in a juice extractor, liquidiser or by nifty handiwork. However you do this, make sure that you have all the juice and that skin and pips are left behind. Peel and core the pears and apples and cut them into small dice.

Place all the ingredients in a pan and simmer gently, stirring well, until the sugar has dissolved. Raise the heat a little and cook until the fruit is soft and the conserve has taken on a glazed transparent look, by which time it should have achieved a soft set (see page 36). Do not be tempted to hurry this process by turning the heat too high as the fruit will stick to the bottom of the pan quite easily. Pot, seal and label.

Leave overnight before eating and keep in the fridge once opened.

FRUIT

Green Grape and Mango Pickle

An exotic and delicious pickle that can be expensive to buy for, but is well worth making for special occasions or unusual presents.

FRUIT

MAKES 6 X 375G JARS

1kg seedless green grapes

400g mixed sultanas, seedless raisins and currants

250g crystallised ginger

300g crystallised lime or citron

15g dried chillies

3–6 garlic cloves, peeled

500g tin mangoes

900ml good white wine vinegar

250g white granulated sugar

100g mustard seeds

15g ground ginger

25g sea salt

6 x 375g sterilised jam jars (page 44)

Wash the grapes. Wash the sultanas, currants and raisins. Chop the ginger and lime or citron and put the chillies and peeled garlic through a mincer or finely chop. Drain the tin of mangoes, making sure that all surplus moisture is removed, and cut into pieces. Pour the vinegar into a large saucepan with the sugar and heat gently, stirring well, until it has dissolved. Boil for 10 minutes and then add the remainder of the ingredients, except the mangoes. Bring to the boil, stirring continuously, reduce the heat and simmer for a further 20–25 minutes, still giving an occasional stir. Add the mangoes and boil for another 5 minutes. Pot, seal and label.

Keep for 1 month before using. Store in a cool, dry place.

Vivien's grapes in Muscat

This is the most delicious way to preserve grapes and absolutely fabulous served after a good dinner.

MAKES 4 X 500ML JARS

1kg seedless green grapes

zest of ½ lemon

200ml white wine vinegar

400ml Muscat or sweet white wine

200g mild-flavoured honey

150g white granulated sugar

10 peppercorns

4 x 500ml sterilised Kilner jars (page 44)

Wash and pat dry the grapes and snip them from the stem, leaving a small piece of stalk. Grate the zest from half the lemon. Put the vinegar, wine, honey, sugar and lemon zest into a pan with the peppercorns. Bring to the boil, stirring to dissolve the sugar, and then simmer until the syrup has reduced by half. Pack the grapes into the jars and tap them down to ensure that they are well packed. Pour the hot syrup over the grapes until they are covered.

Seal tightly, sterilise for 20 minutes (see page 44–5) and label.

Keep for at least 1 month before using. Keep in the fridge once opened.

GRAPEFRUIT

Most people think of grapefruit as the perfect breakfast food – refreshing, non-fattening, full of vitamin C and easily available. However, the grapefruit has hidden talents as it makes the most beautiful tangy preserves and marmalade. There are several varieties of grapefruit, from the very thick-skinned to the thin-skinned and juicy, but one of the best is the pink-fleshed grapefruit, which is full of juice and superbly sweet. For the purposes of these recipes, 4 large grapefruit of the thin-skinned variety weigh approximately 1kg.

Grapefruit and Orange Jam

A sharp and most refreshing jam for those who do not care for the peel in marmalade. The same jam can be made with Seville oranges, which will guarantee a cheery start to the day.

MAKES 2 X 375G JARS

2 large thin-skinned grapefruit

3 large thin-skinned oranges

1 lime

450g white granulated sugar

2 x 375g sterilised jam jars (page 44)

Boil up a large pan of water and drop the grapefruit and oranges into this. Leave for 2 minutes and then peel them – the skin will come off easily, bringing the pith with it. Working over a large dish to catch the juices, cut the flesh of the fruit into small pieces, carefully discarding all the membrane, pips and paper-fine skin. Collect all the juices and put them into a pan. Grate the rind from the lime, extract the juice and add both to the pan with the sugar. Heat gently, stirring until the sugar has dissolved. Bring to the boil and add the flesh from the fruit, then bring to a steady boil, stirring frequently, until a set is obtained (see page 36). Pot, seal and label.

This preserve can be eaten the next day. Store in a cool, dry place.

Grapefruit and Tangerine Jelly

Apart from being good on bread and butter, this very refreshing jelly is unusual and imaginative in a sponge sandwich. Tangerines have a unique and powerful taste, which reduces the astringent flavour of the grapefruit.

MAKES 4 X 375G JARS

4 large thin-skinned grapefruit

500g tangerines

4 lemons

white granulated sugar, warmed (page 17)

muslin or jelly bag

4 x 375g sterilised jam jars (page 44)

Wash the fruit and chop it up. If you have a chop-chop machine, I would suggest that you use it because it cuts the peel into smaller pieces, which will save time for it to soften in the cooking process. Put all the fruit and juices into a large bowl with 5 litres water, cover

FRUIT

and leave to stand overnight.

The next day, transfer the mixture to a large pan and simmer until the peel is really soft (approximately 2 hours). Turn into a muslin or jelly bag and leave to drain overnight into a china bowl. Do not prod or squeeze or the jelly will be cloudy. Measure the juices and for each 600ml gained, take 450g warmed sugar. Return the juice to the pan, bring to the boil and add the sugar, stirring well until it has dissolved. Bring to the boil again and boil hard until a set is obtained (see page 36). Pot, seal and label.

This preserve can be eaten the next day. Store in a cool, dry place.

GREENGAGE

A very underrated member of the plum family that is a superb dessert fruit. It is a sad fact, however, that most of the greengages that come into the shops are as hard as bullets and frequently deteriorate before they ripen. If you can manage to buy greengages from local produce shops, they make such good eating that they do not hang around long enough to be cooked. Preserves made with this green or golden yellow fruit have a sharp sweetness, an attractive colourful appearance and, because of the reasonably high pectin content, set well.

Greengage and Red Gooseberry Jam

This is a very old-fashioned recipe that still works very well.

MAKES 3 X 375G JARS

500g firm greengages

1kg gooseberries

750g white granulated sugar, warmed (page 17)

3 x 375g sterilised jam jars (page 44)

Wash the greengages, remove stalks and stones and put them to one side.

Wash the gooseberries and put them into a pan with 600ml water, cover and cook gently for about 30 minutes, depending on the variety used, until soft, mashing well to break up the fruit more easily. Strain through a sieve. Do not worry if the nameless variety of gooseberry that you have chosen does not give a red juice, either trail a stick of rhubarb through it or be happy with green jam – it will still be delicious.

Put the greengages into the pan with the gooseberry juice and bring gently to the boil, then simmer until the fruit is very soft, the syrup thick and the jam takes on a glossy translucent appearance. Add the warmed sugar and heat gently, stirring well, until the sugar has dissolved. Bring to the boil and boil hard until a set is obtained (see page 36). Pot, seal and label.

This preserve can be eaten the next day. Store in a cool, dry place.

Greengage and Marigold Jelly

A remarkably pretty jelly with a fresh and tangy flavour.

MAKES 6 X 175G JARS

1kg greengages

white granulated sugar, warmed (page 17)

2 lemons

50g marigold petals

muslin or jelly bag

6 x 175g sterilised jam jars (page 44)

Wash and halve the greengages and put them in a pan with 300ml water. Cover and simmer on a low heat until the fruit is disintegrating and is very soft, adding a little more water if necessary. Turn into a muslin or jelly bag and leave to drain overnight into a clean bowl. The next day, measure the juice and for each 600ml, take 450g warmed sugar.

Return the juice to the clean pan, heat gently and add the sugar and lemon juice. Bring slowly to boiling point, stirring continuously to ensure that the sugar has dissolved. Boil until the setting point is reached (see page 36) and remove from the heat for 10 minutes.

Whilst you are waiting for the jelly to cool, pick and prepare the marigold petals, making sure that they are dry, clean and free from insects. Stir them into the jelly to give an even distribution. Pot, seal and label when cold.

Keep for 24 hours before using. Store in a cool, dry place.

LEMONS

It has been said that lemons, honey, garlic and olive oil will protect man from all the ills of mind, body, spirit and soul. Lemon in the most basic way fulfils these promises for they are full of health-giving vitamin C and are of enormous importance to the housewife and cook. To the home preserver, they are an indispensable and invaluable friend – the high pectin/acid content will ensure a set in the most lackadaisical preserve and the acidity will prevent discolouration and give sharpness and life to oversweet or sad jams and jellies. The peel is full of aromatic oils and a mere strip added to pickles gives a tangy pungency that is indefinable. The pith, however, should be treated with caution for it is very bitter and unless used with discretion, can obliterate or change the character of the preserve completely. Lemon juice will alter the flavour of a delicate fruit and will improve the flavour of a dull one. Your choice of lemon should be governed by the thickness of the skin, firmness and bright golden colour.

A few worthwhile pieces of information to help you:

- Many pickle recipes require that you leave lemon skins in salt to soften and lose their bitterness. If you have kept your lemons in the fridge for 24 hours beforehand, or if the whole lemon has been deep frozen, then this process will not take so long. Also the time given for macerating in the jar can be reduced for the peel will soften more rapidly. When lemons are sliced and sprinkled with salt, cover them and leave in the fridge.
- The flavour of lemon juice kept in the fridge for more than a few hours will change.
- Do not use commercial lemon juice with additives as a substitute for the pure juice.
- 6 large or 8–9 small lemons should equal 1kg.
- There are approximately 3 tablespoons of lemon juice

and 1 level tablespoon of grated rind to 1 large, thin-skinned lemon.

- When a dash of lemon juice is required, roll the lemon in your hands to soften it a little, pierce it with the tines of a fork, squeeze out the desired amount of juice and pop it back into the fridge for the next time you need it. Far less wasteful than cutting.
- Zest is the finely grated lemon peel.

Lemon and Sweet Orange Preserve

Do make sure that the lemons you use are thin-skinned and with very little pith. To ensure that the lemon skins are soft, it is a good idea to pop the lemons into a freezer overnight and allow them to defrost before preparing. This cuts down the cooking time. Of course you could put the whole caboodle of lemons and oranges into a chop-chop machine, which will give you a chunkier preserve. This is a lovely fresh preserve with a spicy sweetness.

MAKES 6 X 375G JARS

1kg ripe thin-skinned lemons

500g thin-skinned sweet oranges

1 lime

2 teaspoons crushed coriander seeds

2.75kg white granulated sugar, warmed (page 17)

small muslin bag for spices and pips

6 x 375g sterilised jam jars (page 44)

Wash the fruit and, working on a large dish to catch the juices, cut the lemons and oranges into very thin slices, discarding the nobbly bits at the ends. Collect all the pips and tie them into a muslin bag with the crushed coriander seeds. Grate the zest from the lime and extract the juice.

Put the fruits, juices, muslin bag and 3.5 litres water into a large bowl, cover and leave to stand overnight. The next day, transfer the contents of the bowl to a pan and simmer gently for 2 hours, by then the peels should be soft. Retrieve the muslin bag, giving it a good squeeze. Add the warmed sugar, stirring well until dissolved, and then bring to the boil. Boil hard until it has set (see page 36). Allow the marmalade to cool a little and give it a good stir before potting. Seal and label when cold. This can be eaten the next day. Store in a cool, dry place.

Old-Fashioned Lemon Curd

Homemade curds are delightful and a totally different preserve from the citrus-flavoured sweet paste of commercial products, but they do not keep for longer than 2 months and should be kept in the fridge.

MAKES 4 X 375G JARS

1kg good-quality lemons

225g unsalted butter

900g caster sugar

4 large fresh eggs

4 x 375g sterilised jam jars (page 44)

Wash the lemons and grate the rind finely, taking care to avoid the pith. Extract the juice and sieve it through a fine mesh. Cut the butter into small pieces and put it into a china basin or a double boiler with the sugar, rind and juice. Heat the bowl over a pan of hot water in the fashion of a bain-marie to prevent the bottom of the bowl coming into direct contact with the heat. Stir well with a wooden spoon until the contents are melted and blended.

Beat the eggs, strain them through a sieve and add them to the mixture, beating continuously. Keeping the heat very low and stirring all the time, cook for 30-45 minutes until the mixture is very thick and creamy and adheres to the back of a metal spoon. Watch carefully to see that it does not curdle as there is no way to put this expensive mistake right and once it goes, it goes, and you have scrambled eggs. If the curd shows the slightest tendency to separate, whip the pan off the heat and beat vigorously until you are back on track, then reduce the heat fractionally. Pot, seal and label.

This curd can be eaten the next day. Store in the fridge and use within 2 months.

Curds can be made with other citrus fruits and fruit purées, such as apricots and gooseberries. It is important that these purées are made with the minimum amount of water – 50ml to 1kg fruit. Add the purée to the butter in the same way as the lemons are added and continue as for the curd recipe.

Preserved Lemons

This is such a useful recipe to use when cooking Middle Eastern and North African dishes and as an accompaniment to curries. Should you ever be able to obtain the small bitter green lemons or limes, then you will have another startlingly different combination.

MAKES 2 X 500ML JARS

1kg small thin-skinned lemons

2 tablespoons sea salt

2 teaspoons paprika

sunflower oil (or any fine, flavourless oil)

2 x 500ml sterilised Kilner or similar wide-necked jars with a good seal (page 44)

Wash and slice the lemons, put them into a large colander, sprinkle well with salt and place the colander on a large plate. Cover with a cloth and leave in the fridge for 24 hours. Shake well to remove excess salt and juices and pack into the jars, sprinkling with paprika as you go, then cover completely with the oil.

Seal and label and leave in a warm place until the rind is soft and well macerated, which usually takes about 1 month.

Bitter Lemon Pickle

A very hot accompaniment to very hot dishes.

MAKES 1 X 1.5 LITRE JAR

6 large thin-skinned lemons

2 tablespoons sea salt

6 garlic cloves, peeled

3 fresh chillies

25g fresh ginger, peeled

1 litre sunflower or any fine, flavourless oil

1 x 1.5 litre wide-necked sterilised jar with a good seal (page 44)

Wash the lemons and cut them into wedges lengthways. Salt them all over (to my mind the best way of doing this is to put them with the salt into a polythene bag and give it a good shake). Pack them into the jar, cover and leave to stand in a warm place for 4 days.

Mince the garlic, chillies and ginger and mix them through the lemons. Put the oil in a saucepan and heat it until very hot. Pour carefully over the lemons, doing this slowly to ensure the minimum of air bubbles. Cover tightly and leave for another few weeks before broaching.

Bitter Lemon Chutney

The very best pickle I know – electrifyingly pungent and aromatic without being harsh. An absolutely perfect accompaniment to cold lamb.

MAKES 3 X 375G JARS

1kg thin-skinned lemons

2 tablespoons sea salt

450g yellow sultanas

25g fresh ginger, peeled

4 garlic cloves

25g homemade horseradish or pre-prepared horseradish 'au natural'

300ml cider vinegar

675g soft light brown sugar

1 teaspoon chilli powder

3 x 375g sterilised jam jars (page 44)

Wash the lemons and, working on a large dish, cut into eighths lengthways, removing the pips as you go. Sprinkle with the salt and leave in the fridge for 2 days, turning over and giving a good stir now and again.

Wash and dry the sultanas, peel the ginger if necessary, peel the garlic and wash and scrape the horseradish. Drain the lemons, reserving the liquid. Put all the ingredients through a coarse mincer and transfer them into a large pan. Add the lemon liquid, vinegar, sugar and chilli powder. Mix well and heat gently, stirring all the time. When the sugar has dissolved, bring to the boil and simmer until thick and soft. Pot, seal and label.

Keep for 2 months before using. Store in a cool, dry place.

Lemon and Lime Chutney

Use a food processor to make this simple chutney.

MAKES 3 X 375G JARS

4 thin-skinned lemons

5 limes

150g onions

1 small red chilli

1 small green chilli

150g yellow sultanas

25g mustard seeds

50g sea salt

450g caster sugar

900ml cider vinegar

3 x 375g sterilised jam jars (page 44)

Wash and thinly pare the rind from the lemons and limes with a potato peeler. Extract the juice and reserve. Peel the onions and cut into quarters. Put the rinds with the onions, chillies and sultanas into the bowl of a blender and chop until they form very fine pieces. Scrape this mixture into a saucepan and add the collected juices, mustard seeds, salt, sugar and vinegar. Bring to the boil and stir well until the sugar has dissolved. Reduce the heat and simmer for approximately 2 hours or until the mixture is soft and thick. Pot, seal and label.

Leave for 8 weeks before opening, by which time it will be soft and fierce.

Lemon Barley Water

Best ever refresher for invalids and children on hot days. The same recipe can be made with oranges or a mixture of both fruit. Unless steri- lised (see page 44), it will not keep long and is best kept in the fridge and drunk quite quickly.

MAKES 2 X 1 LITRE OR 4 X 500ML BOTTLES

50g pearl barley

2 large juicy lemons

10 lumps of cube sugar – brown or white

2 x 1 litre or 4 x 500ml sterilised bottles (page 44)

Wash the barley and put it in a pan with 2.25 litres water. Pare the rind from the lemons with a potato peeler and put this with the juice from the lemons into a large bowl and add the sugar. Bring the water and the barley slowly to the boil and then simmer for 10 minutes. Pour the contents of the pan into the bowl, stir well and leave until quite cold. Strain and bottle.

LIMES

Limes are similar to lemons in as much as that they are a small, sharp citrus fruit, but there the resemblance ends for they are smaller with much more acid than lemons and are almost inedible when raw. They have a glorious fragrant smell and taste, which differs totally from the lemon. If a recipe calls for lemon rind or peel and you wish to substitute lime, do so in lesser quantities and the result will be amazingly different. When adapting lemon pickle recipes to use limes, reduce the amount of salt used otherwise the result may be overwhelming. Also, the rinds of limes soften more rapidly than other citrus fruit, therefore the macerating or cooking time should be reduced accordingly. Most lemon recipes can be adapted for limes, but in its own right this rather lovely little fruit makes the most delicious marmalades and pungent pickles to say nothing of refreshing drinks and excellent flavourings. There should be approximately 8–10 limes to 1kg.

Indian Limes

A perfect colourful pickle for those with a penchant for curries, which is difficult and expensive to obtain in the shops. Lemons may be substituted for the limes to make a very different pickle.

MAKES 1 X 1 LITRE JAR

1 litre sunflower oil

1kg fresh limes

1 tablespoon dried shredded chillies

2 tablespoons ground black pepper

1 tablespoon cumin seeds

3 tablespoons sea salt

4 garlic cloves

2.5cm piece of fresh ginger

1 tablespoon lightly crushed white mustard seeds

3 bay leaves

muslin

1 x 1 litre wide-necked sterilised jar, large enough to accommodate all the limes (page 44)

Heat the oil in a saucepan, bringing it up to the point when it begins to smoke, then reduce the temperature right down – just enough to keep it hot – for 10 minutes. Remove from the heat and allow to cool.

FRUIT

Wash the limes and, working on a large dish, cut them into sturdy eighths or quarters, depending upon their size, and place them in a shallow dish with their juices. Put the chillies in a mortar with the pepper, cumin and salt and crush as finely as possible, then sprinkle over the limes and leave for 15 minutes. In the meantime, peel and finely chop the garlic and peel and grate the ginger (if you cannot buy fresh ginger, substitute 1 teaspoon ground ginger). Add the garlic, ginger and mustard seeds to the limes and leave for a further 15 minutes.

Fill the jar with the limes and spices, adding the bay leaves as you go. Pour in the cool oil, cover with muslin and leave to macerate on a sunny windowsill for 1 week, giving it a good shake twice a day.

Cover the top with a piece of clingfilm or a lid as you do this to avoid spillage. Seal tightly and leave in a cool, dry, dark cupboard for 4 weeks before broaching.

MANDARIN

A small orange-type fruit, full of juice, thin-skinned and pithless with firm segments. The flavour of the mandarin is different, but no less distinctive, than a tangerine, but more exciting than clementines and satsumas. It has poor setting qualities, but it makes a light jammy preserve and mouthwateringly good spiced fruits. One of the great advantages of all these little oranges is that, in one guise or another, they are readily available throughout the year. Tangerines, satsumas, calamondins and ortaniques can all be treated in the same way, although the taste varies.

Mandarin and Apricot Preserve

A very delicious mixture.

MAKES 6 X 375G JARS

450g plump dried apricots

1kg mandarins or tangerines

2 large thin-skinned juicy lemons

white granulated sugar, warmed (page 17)

6 x 375g sterilised jam jars (page 44)

If your apricots need to be soaked to make them ready for cooking, then place in a large bowl with enough water for expansion and leave them for several hours. When they have plumped up, drain them and discard the water.

Wash the mandarins in hot water. Remove the pips and cut the fruit into chunks, skin and pulp together, throw into a blender and whizz well until the peel looks finely chopped. If you do not have a blender, then chop by hand or mince. Place the fruit in a deep bowl with 300ml water. Extract the juice from the lemons and add it to the mandarins. Chop up the apricots and add them to the bowl. Leave to soak for a further hour, then measure and for every 450ml fruit and water, take 375g warmed sugar. Transfer the whole caboodle of fruit to a heavy-based pan and simmer gently over a low heat, stirring frequently, until the peel looks soft. Add the sugar to the pan and continue to heat, stirring gently, until it has dissolved. Bring to the boil and boil vigorously, stirring constantly, until the fruit takes on that lovely glistening look and a set is obtained (see page 36). Pot, seal and label.

This preserve can be eaten the next day. Store in a cool, dry place.

Mandarin and Lime Marmalade

One of the loveliest of marmalades with a sharp, fruity, fragrant taste. Using tangerines instead of mandarins makes a completely different preserve.

MAKES 6 X 375G JARS

1kg mandarins

2 large lemons

4 limes

900g white granulated sugar, warmed (page 17)

small muslin bag for pips

6 x 375g sterilised jam jars (page 44)

Wash all the fruit and squeeze out the juices. Remove the pips and tie them into a muslin bag. Either shred the rinds very finely, removing the fruit pulp as you work, or put the whole fruit through a mincer or processor. Place the rind, fruit pulp, muslin bag and juice into a preserving pan with 1.75 litres water and bring to the boil. Simmer until the peel is nicely soft – this can take up to 2 hours. Add the warmed sugar, stirring well until it has dissolved. Bring to the boil and boil hard until a set is obtained (see page 36). Leave to cool and stir well before potting. Seal and label when cold.

This preserve can be eaten the next day. Store in a cool, dry place.

Spiced Mandarins

Small oranges, ortaniques, tange-rines, clementines and satsumas can all be used for this recipe.

MAKES 1 X 1 LITRE OR 2 X 500G JARS

15 mandarins

570ml white wine vinegar

5cm piece of cinnamon

2 teaspoons whole cloves

6 blades mace

1kg white granulated sugar

1 x 1 litre or 2 x 500g wide-necked sterilised jars (page 44)

Slice the mandarins into 1cm slices without peeling them. Lay them in a large pan and just cover with water. Simmer, covered, until the peel is tender – approximately ½ hour. Take off the heat.

Into another large pan, put the vinegar, spices and sugar and bring to the boil, making sure that the sugar has dissolved, then boil hard for 5 minutes. Using a slotted spoon, remove the mandarin slices carefully and lay them in the syrup, making sure that they are well covered. Do not discard the hot water from the first pan because if the syrup does not cover the fruit completely, a little of the boiling liquid can be added. Cover and simmer gently until the mandarins become transparent(ish). Be careful not to overdo this because the fruit can easily fall apart. Remove from the heat and leave overnight.

The next day, boil up gently for 5 minutes, then transfer the mandarin slices to the jars and keep warm. Boil the syrup up until it is thick and gooey and reduced by at least half. When it is thick and gooey then, pour it over the fruit to cover, making sure that there are no air bubbles. Seal, label and leave for 3 months before broaching.

MANGO

Mango can be deliciously succulent, but it is like 'the little girl with the little curl', when it's good, it's very, very good, but when it's bad, it's horrid! I believe that this has to do with the quality of the tree but, nonetheless, a good mango should be plump and firm and when of perfect ripeness, the skin yellow-green with a red blush and the flesh pinky yellow. Mangoes have a high vitamin A and sugar content, which makes them a valuable fruit when raw. When making fresh mango jam or chutney, be careful not to overcook because they can put a very nasty edge on the teeth. Tinned mangoes are frequently used in recipes, but as they are softer, they should not be cooked for so long. Always drain off the syrup unless otherwise stated and do not sprinkle tinned fruit with salt as some recipes require. One mango can weigh between 150–675g, so for 1kg you may need only two fruit, although it is usually only the smaller fruit that is imported.

Mango Preserve

A very attractive preserve. I prefer to use redcurrant juice as it is sharp against the sweetness. Try to remember not to cook mangoes for too long as they can deteriorate into a rather abrasive mash if mishandled.

MAKES 4 X 375G JARS

2 large mangoes, weighing approximately 1kg
white granulated sugar
150ml fresh redcurrant, apple or gooseberry juice
4 x 375g sterilised jam jars (page 44)

Peel and cut the mangoes into even slices, weigh them and for each 500g, take 500g sugar. Put the sugar and 150ml water into a preserving pan and, stirring well, bring to the boil and continue boiling until a thick syrup is formed that will drip very slowly from a spoon. Add the fruit juice and boil for a

FRUIT

further 2 minutes. Add the fruit and bring to the boil again, boiling steadily until the fruit is tender without disintegrating and the syrup is as thick as possible. Allow to cool, then stir well before potting. Seal and label when cold.

This preserve can be eaten the next day. Store in a cool, dry place.

Mango Relish

A colourful and spicy relish that sounds much more expensive than it is. A good recipe to make in the winter.

MAKES 3 X 375G JARS

75g dried figs

75g block dates

175g black raisins

2 garlic cloves

25g fresh ginger

4 small fresh green chillies

2 cardamom pods

2 juniper berries

1 teaspoon green peppercorns

2 teaspoons grated horseradish

150ml white malt vinegar

175g seedless green grapes

1 thin-skinned orange

1 thin-skinned lemon

1 teaspoon sea salt

300g white or light golden granulated sugar

400g tin mangoes

3 x 375g sterilised jam jars (page 44)

Wash and chop the figs and chop the dates and place both in a large china bowl with the raisins.

Peel and chop the garlic and ginger and shred the chillies. Take the seeds from the cardamom pods and crush them with the juniper berries and green peppercorns. Put all the spices and horseradish into the bowl of fruit with the vinegar and mix well. Cover and leave to stand overnight.

The next day, halve the grapes, discarding any pips, and wash and very thinly slice the orange and lemon, working over a large plate to catch the juices. Place all the ingredients except the sugar and mangoes into a large pan, cover and cook very gently until soft. Add the sugar, stirring well until it has dissolved, bring to the boil and simmer for about 40 minutes until thick. In the meantime, drain and chop the mangoes. Add them to the relish 5 minutes before the end of the cooking – this is best judged by the mixture being very soft and thick with very little moisture. Stir well. Pot, seal and label.

Keep for 1 month before using. Store in a cool, dry place.

MINCEMEAT

Mincemeat was originally a mixture of mead, honey, available fruit, meal, spices, beef or mutton and fat, all of which were cooked to a porridge-like consistency, fermented to taste and served on high days and holidays. In time it gradually transformed itself into puddings and pies, some made with sweet mincemeat, others as a savoury filling for pasties and tarts, and many of these exist today in one form or another. Mincemeat has certainly kept its popularity, but it is usually saved for Christmas time to fill short or puff pastry pies. I find that it is often better to make two different kinds of mincemeats – one full of extravagances for special occasions and one that children will like. Shop around for reasonably priced candied peel and nuts, which can be bought in varying qualities from wholefood shops. Whole candied peel is much nicer than the ready chopped, whilst broken nuts are equally as good as whole ones. Do not, however, be tempted to use peanuts, they taste really manky and might upset your guests' health. Fresh beef suet is considered to be the very best to use, but it is not easy to obtain and also takes some wrestling with to get it ready for grating. Most people choose the ready grated or prefer vegetarian suet. Use plenty of juice and alcohol to keep moist, but do not allow it to become soggy. If mincemeat dries out after keeping, it can be swiftly resuscitated with a slug of alcohol – the same applies to the cook at Christmas time.

A final word about the making. When I was first married I lacked a mincer or a grater and I was driven to prepare and make my mincemeat using only a knife, wooden spoon and rolling pin. Chopping, pounding, battering and beating I macerated my mince by hand, but the mincemeat still stands out as the finest that I ever made. Might I suggest that you do yourself a favour and use the chop-chop machine. Your homemade mincemeat will still be miles better than anything bought from the shop. These are two very different recipes, which should give you a good idea of the variations possible.

Traditional Christmas Mincemeat

A delicious Christmas treat.

MAKES 7 X 375G JARS

2 large, hard Bramley apples

1 orange

1 lemon

500g suet

500g raisins (Lexia or Muscatel)

500g yellow sultanas

450g currants

100g mixed nuts (without peanuts)

250g candied peel (citron, orange and lemon)

100g glacé cherries

50g each of glacé pineapple, crystallised ginger and preserved angelica

350g soft light brown sugar

½ teaspoon each of sea salt, fresh grated nutmeg and ground mixed spice

200ml brandy, rum or sherry

7 x 375g sterilised jam jars (page 44), wax discs, brown paper and string

Peel and core the apples. Grate the rind from the orange and lemon and extract the juice. Finely shred the suet if this has not been done for you. Clean the dried fruit if necessary (although most dried fruit is pre-cleaned nowadays). Chop the nuts and the peel finely, followed by the cherries, pineapple, ginger and angelica. Chop the raisins and put the sultanas and currants through a coarse mincer with the apples. Place all the mouthwatering ingredients, except the alcohol, in a large basin and mix well with the orange and lemon juice. Cover and leave overnight.

The next day, stir in the alcohol, making sure that everything is well mixed. Pot, seal with wax discs that have been dipped in brandy and brown paper tied down with string and label.

Keep for 1 month before using. Store in a cool, dry place.

Tarvey House Mincemeat

This recipe was sent to me years ago from a reader whose address was Tarvey House. The mincemeat is different because it has lots more fruity, nutty, sweet additions than usual. A very unusual recipe, which I find that youngsters like.

MAKES 6 X 375G JARS

675g crisp cooking apples

3 sweet oranges

500g currants

500g seedless raisins

225g sultanas

175g glacé cherries

175g whole candied peel

100g dried figs

100g dried, sticky bananas
(not banana chips)

75g hazelnuts

75g toasted almonds

350g suet

2 level teaspoons mixed spice

350g soft dark brown sugar

300ml sherry – sweet or dry

6 x 375g sterilised jam jars (page 44), wax
discs, brown paper and string

Peel and coarsely grate the apples. Finely grate the rind from the oranges and extract the juice. Clean the currants, raisins and sultanas if necessary. Quarter the cherries and very finely chop the peel. Chop the figs and bananas into small pieces and chop the nuts. Grate the suet, if you have not bought pre-prepared, taking care to remove all the stringy bits.

Put all the ingredients except the alcohol into a large china bowl, cover and stir the mincemeat twice daily for 3 days (this gives the fruit time to absorb all the delicious juices before potting). Add the plonk and give the mixture a very good stir before potting. Press the mixture down very well to exclude any air. Seal with wax discs dipped in a little brandy, then tie down firmly with brown paper covers and label.

Keep for 1 month before using. Store in a cool, dry place.

ORANGES

When we talk about oranges, we generally speak in terms of sweet oranges or those suitable for dessert or culinary purposes and bitter oranges, those that are used for making marmalade and that have specialised culinary values. Sweet oranges originally came from Asia, but as they developed a climatic tolerance they became established throughout Europe and the Mediterranean. During the seventeenth and eighteenth centuries, a considerable vogue

FRUIT

arose in Britain amongst the owners of conservatories for possessing the beautiful orange tree with glossy leaves and headily perfumed blossoms and although the fruit was a considerable luxury, it became popular amongst the fashionable. Nowadays, the demand for oranges and the improvements in transport and storage have ensured a constant supply of fruit throughout the year. The vitamin C content in oranges is enormously high, as are the pectin and acid content, therefore they make very satisfactory preserves. Sweet oranges are usually saved for the more elegant conserves and jellies, summery curds and light sweet marmalades.

There are three main types of sweet oranges:

Navel oranges

These have a bumpy little protuberance at one end, hence the name. The rind is usually thick and the flesh of good flavour and nearly always seedless. The downside is that they cannot be guaranteed to be juicy.

Blood oranges

As the name implies, these have a fiery red flesh, which deepens as the fruit ripens.

Common oranges

This description covers a great variety of oranges from different areas. Some of the more familiar are Valencia, Maroc and Jaffa. The thickness of peel, the quantity of juice and degree of sweetness all vary considerably and there is no way of guessing how good an orange is. A great deal also depends on how ripe they were when picked and how long they have been in transportation and storage.

Bitter or Seville oranges

These made their appearance originally in Southern Europe. They are a much hardier tree and may even be grown on a south-facing wall in frost-free, sunny areas of Britain. Bitter oranges make the traditional tangy marmalades and are virtually unsuitable for any other preserves, although the peel and juice make exceptional flavourings for savoury dishes. It is a good idea to freeze a few Seville oranges when they come on the market (they freeze very well for a short period of time) for they are invaluable in certain sauces as the flavour is unique and cannot be copied with sweet oranges. Seville oranges can be recognised as a fruit with a deep orange, pitted skin of sharp and bitter tastes. The flesh and juice are sour and unpalatable when raw. A fresh orange, which has not been kept from the previous year, should not feel dry and empty when pressed, but firm to the touch.

Bergamot

An orange that is primarily used in the perfume industry for its rind, which contains invaluable aromatic oils.

Orange blossom

Used to make orange flower water, which is frequently used in more delicate preserves.
It is always advisable to wash oranges in warm water, even scrubbing them gently with a soft brush, as they are often sprayed to improve their colour or for storage. The weight of oranges is very hard to gauge as they vary considerably in size and thickness of pith and this guide is only approximate: 5 large thick-skinned Jaffas will weigh 1kg, but for a good preserve you will need to use an orange with a thinner skin and less pith. Seven medium thin-skinned oranges should make up to 1kg.

A Bitter Orange Jelly

A really lovely sharp and tangy preserve, equally good as a sweet or savoury. A very pretty and aromatic idea is to add a scented geranium leaf to a half pot of jelly and leave for a moment or two before filling. It should stay suspended as the pot is filled.

MAKES 4 X 375G JARS

500g Seville oranges

500g sweet thin-skinned oranges

3 lemons

1 grapefruit

white granulated sugar, warmed (page 17)

muslin or jelly bag

4 x 375g sterilised jam jars or twice that
amount of small jars (page 44)

Wash the fruit and, working on a
large dish, cut into small pieces. Put
all the pulp, peel and rind with any
collected juices into a large pan,
add 2 litres water and cook until the
contents are reduced by half. To save
time and money, if you own a large
slow cooker that will accommodate
this quantity, then put all the fruit and
juices into it and add hot water. Cook
on high until the peel is soft and the
contents reduced. Turn the contents
of the pan into a muslin or jelly bag
and leave to drain overnight without
prodding. The next day, measure the
juice gained and for each 600ml, take
500g warmed sugar. Return the juice
to a different pan and heat gently, then
add the sugar, stirring hard until it has
dissolved. Bring to the boil and boil
at a steady rolling boil until a set is
achieved (see page 36). Pot, seal
and label.

This preserve can be eaten the next
day. Store in a cool, dry place.

Orange and Basil Jelly

This is a lovely jelly with chicken,
turkey, etc. and because of the
delightful fragrance of basil, it is a
joy to make. Basil may be added to
any of the orange and fruit jellies, but
I feel that bitter oranges with basil
have an aromatic subtlety.

MAKES 8 X 175G JARS

500g bitter or Seville oranges

500g sweet oranges

2 lemons

a large bunch of fresh basil

white granulated sugar, warmed (page 17)

muslin or jelly bag

8 x 175g small sterilised jam jars (page 44)

Wash the fruit and chop the whole lot
(it may help to turn it into a liquidiser),
then put the pulp, peel and juice into
a preserving pan with 3 litres water.
Divide the basil in two, wash well and
add one half to the pan. Cook until all
the fruit is soft and the quantity reduced
by half. Turn into a muslin or jelly bag
and leave to drain overnight into a clean
bowl. The next day, measure the juice
gained and for every 600ml, take 450g
warmed sugar. Return the juice to the
pan, heat gently and add the sugar,

stirring well until it has dissolved. Bring
to the boil and boil hard until a set is
obtained (see page 36).

In the meantime, make sure that the
remaining basil is clean and dry and
chop it very finely. Stir it into the finished
jelly and allow to cool a little before
potting, stirring to disperse the herbs.
Pot, seal and label when cold.

Keep for 2 weeks before using. Store
in a cool, dry place. It is best kept in the
fridge once opened.

Orange Chutney

Hot, thick, sweet and fiery.

MAKES 4 X 375G JARS

1kg sweet oranges

500g hard green apples

2 large onions

25g fresh chillies

225g seedless raisins

225g preserved ginger

50g sea salt

1.15 litres malt vinegar

500g soft brown sugar

4 x 375g sterilised jam jars (page 44)

Wash and peel the oranges,
removing the pith, pips and papery
bits (whilst orange peel is full of
aromatic oils that give the flavour, the pith
can be unpleasantly bitter). Wash, peel
and core the apples. Peel the onions and
deseed the chillies. Now either mince
or chop the orange peel and flesh, the
apples, onions, chillies, raisins and ginger
or you can throw the whole lot into the
chop-chop machine (if you do this, you
should make sure that the orange peel
is in relatively small pieces so that it will
chop up properly). Put this mixture into a
pan with the salt and half the vinegar and
cook for approximately 1 hour until very
soft. Dissolve the sugar in the remaining
vinegar and add this to the pan. Simmer
for about 30 minutes until thick and
cooked. Pot, seal and label.

Keep for 2 months before using. Store
in a cool, dry place.

Orange Liqueur

Best kept well hidden.

MAKES 3 X 600ML BOTTLES

2 large thin-skinned oranges

450g Demerara sugar

2 vanilla pods

1 bottle of vodka

muslin cloth for straining

1 x large sterilised wide-necked jar and 3 x 600ml sterilised decorative bottles or a decanter with tight lids or stoppers (page 44)

Scrub the oranges and peel them thinly, removing any pith. Extract the juice. Put 250ml water into a saucepan with the sugar, heat gently, then boil to a syrup consistency. Remove from the heat and gradually add 250ml more water, stirring well until the syrup has dissolved. Add the peel and orange juice to the syrup with the vanilla pods. When quite cold, stir in the vodka and transfer this alcoholic indulgence to the clean jar. Seal firmly and leave for at least 2 weeks in a cool, dry, dark cupboard. Strain through muslin over a sieve. Bottle, seal and label.

MARMALADE

The origins of marmalade are a little murky. There are those who support the theory that the Portuguese sailors who first discovered the orange believed it to be a quince, hence marmelo, the Portuguese for quince. Maybe it was a corruption of the Greek meli (honey) and melon (apple)? Or could it have been the sweet potted oranges whipped up by a devoted French chef for his ailing mistress, Mary Queen of Scots, hence 'Marie est malade'. Nevertheless, by 1800 marmalade was firmly established due to a strong-minded and resourceful Scotswoman called Mrs Keiller, the wife of a Dundee grocer. Appalled at the apparent mismanagement of her husband who instead of ordering a consignment of sweet oranges received instead Seville oranges, which would not sell, she set about utilising them in such a way as to recoup their losses. Enterprising lady that she was, she established a British devotion to marmalade that exists to this day.

Marmalade is an extraordinary bitter-sweet conserve made of citrus fruits and sugar, which uses the peel, flesh and a percentage of pith to give a mouth-cleansing, tangy result. It can be improved upon and experimented with by the addition of other fruits, candied peels, spices, alcohol, etc, and may be fine and golden; thick, dark and chunky; or purely a jelly, but it should always have the same background bitterness that is unique to marmalade. Seville oranges are the true basis of a good marmalade, but lime, lemon, kumquat and grapefruit all make a good substitute when used in conjunction with sweet oranges.

One thing to remember is that the peel takes a long time to soften, therefore it is a very good idea to leave the prepared fruit standing in the water overnight. This also gives the best pectin extract, thus ensuring a good set. Although when making 'shred' marmalade the peel has to be painstakingly cut into thin slices, you can use the chop-chop machine when making chunky marmalade, although this is not as purist as hand-cutting. Another good method is to soak and cook the fruit, leave until it is cold and then put it into the chop-chop machine, which will give a fine, thick result.

Marmalade made using a pressure cooker

Any marmalade recipe can be made using a pressure cooker. As the firm peel of all citrus fruit can take a long time to soften by conventional methods, this is both economical and time saving. It is important to remember that in order to achieve the best results, the fruit should be soaked for at least 12 hours before cooking. Remember not to overfill the pan – most large pressure cookers will not take more than 2kg of fruit – and as the peel will soften more quickly in a shorter time span, you will need less water than your recipe states – approximately 1.15 litres water to 1kg fruit.

Remove the trivet and place the prepared fruit with the water into the cooker. Cover and bring

FRUIT

to 6.8kg pressure for 10 minutes, remove from the heat and allow the pressure to reduce at room temperature. Continue as for the given recipe, but do not replace the lid once the sugar has been added. Take care not to overcook the fruit because not only will it look unappetising and flaccid, but the pectin content will be impaired.

Marmalade made using a freezer

Seville oranges come into the shops for a very limited and rarely opportune period, so rather than losing the opportunity of homemade marmalade throughout the coming year, buy the oranges and freeze them for future use. Wash them with lukewarm water, dry well and pack into heavy polythene bags, extracting the air and sealing tightly. It is wise to add a few fresh citrus fruit to the mixture when cooking as there may be a small pectin loss. Alternatively, prepare and cook the fruit to the point at which the sugar should be added. This can be done speedily using a blender and pressure cooker. Pack into rigid polythene containers, leaving at least 3cm headroom. Seal, label and freeze. Use as soon as practical.

Test for set

A very good way to test for a set is to place a saucer in the fridge until it is nicely cold, remove the pan of marmalade or jam from the heat and put a small spoonful of the preserve on the saucer. Pop it back in the cold for a few more seconds and then if it wrinkles and is sluggish when pushed, you will know you have a set. Never leave a preserve on the heat as you test for a set as you may bubble past the point of no return.

A good basic Seville Orange Marmalade

A straightforward traditional method.

8 X 375G JARS

1kg Seville oranges

1 lemon

2kg white granulated sugar, warmed
(page 17)
small muslin bag for pips
8 x 375g sterilised jam jars (page 44)

Wash all the fruit and, working over
a large dish, either slice thinly, chop
coarsely or mince it, collecting the pips
and tying them into a muslin bag. Put
this with the juices, fruit and 2.25 litres
water into a deep bowl, cover and
leave to stand for 24 hours. Transfer to
a large pan and simmer gently until
soft and reduced by about half. Add
the warmed sugar, stirring well until it
has dissolved, bring to the boil and boil
hard until a set is obtained (see page
36). Leave to stand for 10 minutes and
stir well. Pot, seal and label when cold.

This preserve can be eaten the next
day. Store in a cool, dry place.

The following ideas may be incorporated into this traditional marmalade:

- To make a strong, bitter
  marmalade, leave the pith on
  the orange peel. For a more
  ladylike result, remove the pith
  and put it in the pip bag.
- Great variations on the flavour
  of marmalade can be obtained
  by your choice of sugar. Soft
  light brown and brown sugar
  give a mellow result. Dark
  brown and muscovado add
  a heavier, richer quality to the
  marmalade, which is
  particularly good when a
  half a cup of alcohol is added
  (brandy, rum and whisky
  spring readily to mind).
  Molasses and black treacle
  can be used in the proportions
  of 2 tablespoons per kilogram
  of fruit to give a darker and
  suitably sinister effect.
- Angelica, chopped and added
  a few minutes before the end
  of cooking, adds a sweet and
  perfumed flavour to any
  marmalade recipe. Preserved
  ginger or well-cut glacé
  orange peel will add its own
  inimitable taste.
- To add a spicy fillip to marmalade,
  either add 1 teaspoon mixed ground
  spice or the spice of your choice
  with the sugar. Alternatively, whole
  spices such as coriander, root
  ginger, cardamom or cloves can be
  crushed and added to the bag of pips.

FRUIT

Orange Shred Marmalade

What a kerfuffle, but worthwhile for those who prefer this kind of marmalade.

MAKES 8 X 375G JARS

1kg Seville oranges

2 lemons

2kg white sugar – preserving or jam sugar gives a clearer result, warmed (page 17)

muslin or jelly bag for straining

8 x 375g sterilised jam jars (page 44)

Wash the fruit and remove the peel or 'zest' from the oranges with a potato peeler, taking care not to take the pith. Cut the peel into very fine shreds and pop it into a pan with 2 litres water. Bring gently to the boil and then simmer until the peel is very soft and the liquid is reduced by half, and reserve this.

Extract the juice from the oranges and lemons and strain it through a thickness of muslin. Coarsely chop the pulp, pips and pith and put them into a large pan with a further 2 litres water, bring to the boil and reduce to a simmer for at least 1 hour or until the mixture looks mushy and soft. Strain through a muslin or jelly bag. Pour the juice from the cooked pulp, the reserved orange and lemon juice and the rind and its liquid into the clean pan. Heat gently and add the warmed sugar, stirring well until it has dissolved. Bring to the boil and boil hard until a set is obtained (see page 36). Leave to cool, stir well and pot (this ensures a good distribution of shreds). Seal and label when cold.

This preserve can be eaten the next day. Store in a cool, dry place.

Dark Marmalade with Rum

Whisky can be incorporated into this recipe instead of rum. Another brilliant idea is to substitute, in part, a bottle of ginger ale for some of the water, leave out the rum and add chopped ginger after the sugar has been added. A lovely ginger marmalade.

8 X 375G JARS

1kg Seville oranges

2 lemons

150ml dark rum

2kg white granulated sugar

5 tablespoons black treacle

small muslin bag for pips

8 x 375g sterilised jam jars (page 44)

Wash the fruit and, working over a large dish to catch the juices, cut into small, coarse chunks or mince coarsely depending on your preference. Collect the pips, tie them into a muslin bag, and place this with prepared fruit, 2.25 litres water and the rum into a deep bowl. Cover and leave for 24 hours.

The next day, transfer the contents of the bowl to a preserving pan and simmer for about 2 hours until very soft. Remove the muslin bag and add the sugar and treacle (the best way to soften and measure the treacle is to stand the treacle tin in a warm oven for a short while and use a cloth to handle it). Stir well until the sugar has dissolved, bring to the boil and boil hard until a set is obtained (see page 36). The marmalade should be very thick. If you feel so inclined, you can always add an extra slug of rum at this point. Leave to stand for 10 minutes before potting. Seal and label when cold.

This preserve can be eaten the next day. Store in a cool, dry place.

Five Fruit Marmalade

A good strong, tasty marmalade. Although the time lapses may seem inconvenient, this method ensures a shorter cooking time and a better flavour. You can adapt this method for any marmalade recipe.

6 X 375G JARS

900g sweet oranges

1 large thin-skinned grapefruit

3 lemons

1 lime

125g kumquats

2kg white granulated sugar, warmed (page 17)

small muslin bag for pips

6 x 375g sterilised jam jars (page 44)

Wash all the fruit well and, working over a large dish, cut into large chunks, removing the pips as you go and tying them into a muslin bag. Although you can take a more purist approach cutting the fruit into tiny pieces by hand, I find that the best way to make this marmalade is to put all of it, pith, peel and flesh, into the chop-chop machine and zizz it fiercely until it is fine. As grapefruit skin is very thick, you might like to give it a bit of zizz first before adding the rest of the fruit.

As it is, you will probably be working in several batches. Place all in a large bowl with the bag of pips and cover fully with water, ensuring that there is at least 7.5cm water above the fruit. Cover with a cloth and leave to stand for 24 hours, by which time the peel should have softened considerably.

Put in a large pan and cook gently until most of the water has evaporated. Remove from the heat, cover and leave for at least another 8 hours. Remove the muslin bag and bring the fruit to a gentle rolling boil, then add the warmed sugar, stirring well until it has dissolved. Continue boiling gently, stirring occasionally, until a set is obtained (see page 36). This is best judged by the marmalade taking on a glowing translucent appearance. Remove the pan from the heat and test for a set. Pot, seal and label. This preserve can be eaten the next day. Store in a cool, dry place.

Kumquat Marmalade

MAKES 2 X 375G JARS

500g kumquats

800g white granulated sugar, warmed (page 17)

2 x 375g small sterilised jam jars (page 44)

Wash and mince the kumquats, discarding the pips and catching any of the escaping juices. Place the fruit in a preserving pan with 300ml water, bring to the boil and simmer for 20 minutes or until the peel looks soft. Add the warmed sugar, stirring constantly until it has dissolved, then boil for a further 30 minutes or so until a set is obtained (see page 36). Pot, seal and label.

This preserve can be eaten the next day. Store in a cool, dry place.

PEACH
An ancient and lovely fruit from China, the garden of civilisation, which flourishes throughout the temperate zones of the world, both as a cultivated fruit and growing wild. The varieties of peaches are endless, from the clingstone where the stone adheres firmly to the flesh of the fruit to the freestone, where it slides easily free. There are white, flat peaches with the merest whiff of perfume as delicate as distant wood smoke and there are great golden

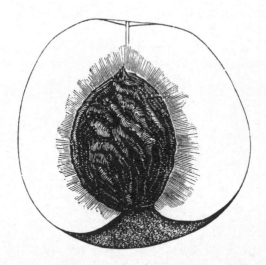

peaches with a rich, full flavour, juicy to the stone. Peaches with a soft grey fuzz and others so deep a red as to be almost purple. Although few of these ancient varieties reach the open market, some may still be grown in warm gardens and sheltered allotments. Town produce markets or produce auctions often have trays of reasonably priced fruit for sale and you can always ask them to get a tray for you. The white peaches make lovely sophisticated preserves, whilst the big, jolly golden giants are best in jams or pickled and spiced. Although it might seem wicked to do this to a really rather expensive fruit, bear in mind that a good fruit, properly preserved, can be an attractive and appetising addition to the menu throughout the year. Nothing can better an elegantly stoppered jar of golden peaches soaked in brandy or a humble salad of crisp Cos lettuce and thin slices of salt beef, brightened by a jar of spiced peaches.

Nectarines are a delicious

FRUIT

FRUIT

FRUIT

FRUIT

smooth-skinned fruit similar to peaches. If you manage to obtain a quantity of ripe nectarines, then treat them as you would peaches and apricots as the recipes are virtually interchangeable.

Both peaches and nectarines need to be skinned before using and the simplest way to do this is to drop into boiling water for 30 seconds, rinse briefly under cold running water and then the skins slip off easily. Peaches do not set with any great degree of success and nearly all recipes will specify the use of much lemon and little water or a high pectin fruit juice. Slightly underripe peaches will make a good jam, but for every 500g fruit, you will need an additional 150ml water and cook the fruit, prior to adding the sugar, very gently and with the lid on.

As peaches are such a delicate and exotic fruit, I think that it is somewhat cavalier to treat them roughly and the following recipes have a more reverend approach.

Fresh Peach Jam using Commercial Pectin

Using commercial pectin ensures that with minimum cooking the fruit keeps its fresh flavour and does not become an unrecognisable mash.

MAKES 3 X 600G JARS

1kg ripe peaches

2 large lemons

1kg white granulated sugar, warmed (page 17)

1 x 250ml bottle of commercial pectin

3 x 600g sterilised wide-necked jam jars (page 44)

Peel the peaches, cut the fruit into thick slices and remove the stones, cracking a few of these and extracting a few kernels to give the connoisseur touch. Squeeze 3 tablespoons of juice from the lemons and put this with the fruit and 600ml water into a large pan. Simmer gently until the peach slices are tender, but not soggy. Add the warmed sugar and stir well until it has dissolved. Bring to the boil and boil rapidly for 2 minutes. Add the pectin, stirring well, and remove the pan from the heat (this ensures that the foam dies down and does not flow over the pan). Add the chopped kernels and skim and stir the jam for 2 minutes. Allow to cool before potting. Seal and label when cold.

Keep for 1 week before using. Store in a cool, dry place.

Peach and Raspberry Preserve

A delicious preserve that makes the best of two luxury fruit. Peaches have no appreciable setting quality and raspberries are not much better, but the addition of lemon juice and the use of natural juices rather than adding water, help to overcome this problem without loss of flavour through overboiling.

MAKES 3 X 375G JARS

900g firm ripe peaches

900g fresh raspberries

juice of 4 lemons

1.5kg white cane sugar

3 x 375g sterilised jam jars (page 44)

Slip the skins from the peaches, quarter and remove the stones. Do not wash the raspberries, but make sure that they are clean and free from creepy crawlies. Place both fruits in a deep bowl with the lemon juice and sugar, mix gently, cover with a cloth and leave to stand overnight, turning once or twice to disperse the sugar.

The next day, pour the contents of the bowl into a large pan and heat gently, stirring well, until there is plenty of juice and the sugar has completely dissolved, then bring to a slow rolling boil. Continue to stir occasionally and watch like a hawk to prevent sticking. It should take about 15 minutes to obtain a soft set (see page 36). Allow to cool a little and stir well before potting. Seal and label when cold.

This preserve can be eaten the next day. Store in a cool, dry place.

Tropical Fruit Jam

A lovely mixture of flavours for the tea table.

MAKES 5 X 375G JARS

500g peaches

225g nectarines

500g fresh apricots

225g prepared pineapple

225g fresh mango flesh

juice of 3 lemons

1.5kg preserving sugar

5 x 375g sterilised jam jars (page 44)

Wash the fruit and slip the skins from the peaches and nectarines. Working over a large dish to catch any juices, cut the peaches, apricots and nectarines into thick slices. Finely dice the pineapple and mango. Place all these prepared fruit in a large saucepan with their juices and the lemon juice and heat gently until there is enough liquid to simmer in.

Bring to the boil, cover and simmer, stirring occasionally, for about 15–30 minutes until the fruits are soft. Remove the lid and add the sugar. Bring to the boil, stirring constantly, until the sugar has dissolved, then boil rapidly until a set is obtained (see page 36). Pot, seal and label.

This preserve can be eaten the next day. Store in a cool, dry place.

Peaches in Brandy Wine

Apricots, nectarines, greengages, Victoria plums and cherries may all be brandied in this fashion. Serve with cream or just as they are in their own syrup for dessert on high days and holidays.

MAKES 1 X 1KG JAR

white granulated sugar

1kg firm white or golden peaches

good-quality brandy

1 x 1kg sterilised wide-necked preserving jar (page 44)

Using a large saucepan, make up a syrup with 500g sugar and 1 litre water. In the meantime, slip the skins from the peaches, cut in half and remove the stones. Small peaches can be left whole, wiped with a damp cloth and pricked through to the stone with a silver needle in order that they may absorb the syrup.

When the thin syrup is ready, slide the peaches into the pan and bring very slowly to the boil, making sure that the fruit is immersed. Once the

FRUIT

boil has been reached, remove the peaches with a slotted spoon and pack into the jar. Measure the syrup and for each 600ml, take 900g sugar. Return the sugar and syrup to the pan and heat gently, stirring well, until the sugar has dissolved. Bring to the boil and boil hard until the syrup will form a thread when pulled up by the spoon. Measure the syrup and take an equal quantity of brandy. Mix well and pour over the fruit to cover. Using a spoon, gently press up and down on the top of the jar, whilst shaking carefully, to remove air bubbles. Seal tightly and label.

The longer you can leave these fruit in a cool, dark place the better, preferably 1 month, but do try to leave for at least 1 week before yielding to luscious temptation..

Peach Chutney

A nicely tangy and aromatic chutney with a bite. This is also a very good recipe in which to utilise underripe peaches.

MAKES 4 X 375G JARS

1kg peaches

2 small white onions

350g golden sultanas

25g fresh ginger

1 lemon

25g yellow mustard seeds

3 teaspoons sea salt

450g Demerara sugar

450ml white malt or cider vinegar

4 x 375g sterilised jam jars (page 44)

Remove the peach skins and stones and chop the peaches. Peel and chop the onions and put them with the peaches into a pan with just enough water to prevent sticking. Cover and cook gently until the peaches are tender. In the meantime, chop the sultanas, peel and shred the ginger into fine pieces and grate the zest from the lemon. Put these ingredients with the mustard seeds, the juice from the lemon and the salt, sugar and vinegar into the pan of peaches. Stir well until the sugar has dissolved, bring to the boil and boil gently for at least 40 minutes until the chutney is thick and soft. Pot, seal and label.

Keep for 1 month before using. Store in a cool, dry place.

FRUIT

PEAR

There are a great many varieties of pears, not only from the British Isles, but also from every temperate area of the world. The original pear, *Pyrus communis*, still grows wild in Britain and Europe, and it is from this scrubby tree with rock-hard green fruit that comes the present majestic dark pear tree, with leaves that may vary from the palest silvery green to a deep autumnal russet and a wood much beloved by the bespoke furniture maker.

A perfect classic pear – Beurre, Comice, Williams, or Williams Bon Chretein to give it its proper name – is the very best dessert fruit you can enjoy, therefore it follows that it would be akin to a sin to cook them unless, of course, you preserve them in brandy. The pears that really lend themselves to jams, pickles and chutneys are the robust Christmas pears or Catillac, Conference, Crassane and Winter Nelis, should you be given the choice, but from wherever your source you need a relatively hard pear with a good flavour. Windfall and good pears are often found at the roadside and, with an abundant crop, tree owners are only too happy to give them away rather than let the wasps have them. Pears have a poor pectin content, but can produce a nice gooey pudding jam.

Devon Pear Conserve

A tasty jam with good spreadable qualities and excellent when used in puddings, for instance a good hefty dollop in the bottom of a steamed or baked sponge pudding or as a sauce on ice cream or milk puddings. If you are feeling Spartan, you can substitute the cider with a good pure apple juice. Economical and delicious.

3 X 375G JARS

1kg well-flavoured pears

150ml sweet cider

675g white granulated sugar, warmed (page 17)

2 lemons

3 x 375g sterilised jam jars (page 44)

Wash and chop the pears very small. Pour the cider into a pan, bring to the boil and add the pears. Simmer until tender enough to mash and put through a sieve or through a blender and then through a sieve. Return the purée to the pan, heat gently and add the warmed sugar, stirring well until it has dissolved. Squeeze the juice from the lemons, add it to the pan, then bring to the boil and boil hard, stirring continuously, for approximately 30 minutes until the conserve takes on a slightly glazed look, although it will rarely form a good set. Pot, seal and label.

This preserve can be eaten the next day. Store in a cool, dry place.

Spiced Pear and Pineapple Jam

A warm and unusual jam, which is a special treat for those cold winter months.

MAKES 4 X 375G JARS

1kg cooking pears
225g prepared pineapple
1 sweet orange and lemon
4 whole cloves
2.5cm piece of dried root ginger
675g white granulated sugar
2 tablespoons sweet sherry (optional)

small muslin bag for spices and pips
4 x 375g sterilised jam jars (page 44)

Peel, core and chop the pears. Chop or grate the pineapple. Grate the rind from the orange and lemon and chop the flesh, making sure that you retain the juices and keep the pips. Bruise the spices and tie them into a muslin bag with the pips. Put all these ingredients into a pan with the juices and sugar and heat very gently, stirring continuously, until the sugar has dissolved and a thin syrup is beginning to form. Bring to the boil and boil for approximately 10 minutes, taking great care not to burn. Remove the spice bag and stir in the sherry, if using, and give it a good stir. Pot, seal and label.

This preserve can be eaten the next day. Store in a cool, dry place.

High Derry Down Conserve

This very well-flavoured conserve is an old-fashioned recipe handed down from a house in Ireland.

MAKES 8 X 375G JARS

1kg windfall or hard apples

1kg cooking pears

500g plums

2 sweet oranges

1 lemon

50g black raisins

1.75kg white preserving sugar, warmed (page 17)

1 tablespoon lemon brandy or Cointreau (optional).

8 x 375g sterilised jam jars (page 44)

Wash, peel, core and chop the apples and pears. Split the plums, removing stones where you can (although this is not essential as they usually bob up during cooking). Grate the rind from the oranges and lemon and extract the juice, and roughly chop the raisins. Put all of these ingredients into a large saucepan with 150ml water, cover and simmer for about 1 hour until just soft. Add the warmed sugar, bring gently to the boil, stirring constantly until the sugar has dissolved, then boil at a rolling boil until the conserve takes on a rich translucent look and a set is obtained (see page 36). Stir in the alcohol, if using. Pot, seal and label.

This preserve can be eaten the next day. Store in a cool, dry place.

Pear Chutney

This is a really lovely traditional chutney that will last for ages and the longer you keep it, the better it gets.

MAKES 10 X 375G JARS

2kg firm pears

750g onions

350g tart apples

200g raisins

35g fresh ginger, peeled

2 garlic cloves, peeled and crushed

15g sea salt

1 lemon

3 small dried chillies

4 whole cloves

⅓ stick of cinnamon

½ teaspoon mustard seeds

500ml white malt vinegar

150g light soft brown sugar

small muslin bag for spices

10 x 375g sterilised jam jars (page 44)

Peel the pears, remove the cores, cut into quarters and then slice each quarter in half. Peel and slice the onions; peel, core and slice the apples and coarsely chop the raisins. Shred the ginger, crush the garlic in the salt, grate the rind and take the juice from half the lemon. Put all these ingredients into a large bowl, mix well, cover and leave to stand for 2 hours.

Shred the chillies, tie the cloves and cinnamon into a muslin bag and place these with the mustard seeds, vinegar and sugar into a large pan. Bring to the boil and boil for 5 minutes. Add the fruit mixture and cook gently, stirring frequently to prevent burning, until the chutney is thick and dark, which can take as long as 3 hours. Remove the spice bag. Pot, seal and label.

Keep for 1 month before using. Store in a cool, dry place.

David's Allotment Chutney

A great way to use up all those odds and ends. Leave for a month or two to mature into a rich, fruity mixture.

MAKES 7 X 375G JARS

450g hard pears

450g windfall apples

450g true quinces

450g onions

225g celery

450g ripe tomatoes

125g Lexia raisins

2 tablespoons pickling spice

1 tablespoon grated fresh ginger

2 teaspoons sea salt

900ml white malt vinegar

450g white granulated sugar

small muslin bag for spices

7 x 375g sterilised jam jars (page 44)

Peel, core and chop the fruit. Peel and slice the onions and chop the celery. Skin and quarter the tomatoes (the best way of skinning tomatoes is to drop them into boiling water and leave for 1 minute, when the skins should then split and slide off easily). Roughly chop the raisins. Tie the pickling spice into a small muslin bag.

Put all these ingredients into a large pan with the ginger, salt and half the vinegar. Bring gently to the boil and simmer for at least 1 hour until very soft, stirring occasionally to prevent the mixture sticking. Remove the muslin bag, add the sugar with the remaining vinegar and keep stirring until the sugar has dissolved. Continue to cook at a gentle boil, stirring from time to time, for 40–60 minutes until the mixture is thick. Pot, seal and label.

Keep for 2 months before using. Store in a cool, dry place.

FRUIT

Your own pear liqueur

This is such an exciting idea that it is worth mentioning. You will need a pear tree, preferably a William, a clear squat glass bottle with a moderately wide neck and some wire. Wait until the blossom has fallen from the tree and tiny fruit are forming, then pick a likely looking candidate. Break off any surplus wood, keeping the fruit on the bough and gently place the baby fruit in the bottle. Tie a wire round the neck of the bottle and attach it to the branch. Block up the opening to prevent insects invading and leave the little fruit to ripen, on the tree, in its own hothouse. When the pear is fully ripe, cut it and the jar from the branch and, keeping it in its glasshouse, take it to the kitchen. Make up a syrup composed of 1 litre vodka to 300g caster sugar. Pierce the pear gently with a thin knitting needle to allow the fruit to absorb the alcohol and, once the sugar has dissolved in the vodka, pour this liquor into the bottle to cover the fruit. Seal tightly and hide away in a cool, dark place for at least 6 months. You may achieve a similar result with a ready-bought William pear and using a wide-necked bottling jar. It's not so much fun though.

PINEAPPLE

A pineapple, that golden, roundly conical fruit surmounted by a tazz of serrated green leaves, is not one fruit, but is made up of many hundreds of small fruit all growing together by some miracle of nature. Many of us might remember trying to grow pineapples from the green top placed in a saucer of water and living in smelly glory on the windowsill. Pineapples are sweet and juicy and full of vitamins A and C. And they make good, if somewhat runny, preserves, losing much of their sharpness in cooking and taking on a mellow flavour and colour. As a large amount of the fruit is bristly skin, leaves and a hard core, it is impossible to gauge an accurate weight without first preparing it. Never use any part of the fruit that is turning brown, for this will cause a fermentation in the finished preserve if kept for any length of time.

FRUIT

Cape Conserve

A delicious combination of summery flavours that came from a South African farming friend, which is cheaply and easily made throughout the winter.

MAKES 5 X 375G JARS

2 tangerines

150ml pure apple juice

600g prepared pineapple

500g cooking apples

450g seedless green grapes

1.25kg white granulated sugar, warmed (page 17)

5 x 375g sterilised jam jars (page 44)

Peel the tangerines, finely shred the skins and put them in a small pan with the apple juice, covering and simmering very gently for about 40 minutes until soft. In the meantime, grate the pineapple onto a large plate, catching the juice as you work. Peel, core and dice the apples. Put both the pineapple and the apple into a preserving pan with 150ml water, the tangerine peel and juices, bring to the boil and simmer for about 20 minutes until soft. Separate the tangerine segments and wash the grapes, removing them from their stalks. Add them both to the pan and simmer for a further 10 minutes. Add the warmed sugar, stirring constantly until it has dissolved. Bring to the boil and boil hard until a set is obtained (see page 36). Although the tangerine pieces separate and disappear, the grapes remain whole, making a very attractive preserve. Allow to cool a little and stir well before potting. Seal and label when cold.

This preserve can be eaten the next day. Store in a cool, dry place.

Pineapple Relish

Dracula might be intimidated by this relish, but friends who are dotty over garlic will love it. The amount of garlic can be reduced, but these proportions do give an exceptional flavour.

MAKES 6 X 375G JARS

1kg prepared pineapple

50g sea salt

8–12 garlic cloves

175g fresh ginger

400g seedless raisins

750ml brown or white malt vinegar, plus a little extra

450g soft light brown sugar

⅛ teaspoon fresh grated nutmeg

Working over a large dish, chop the prepared pineapple flesh, reserving any juices, and sprinkle it with the salt. Leave to stand for 1–2 hours. Peel and mince the garlic and ginger. Mince the raisins. Turn the pineapple into a colander, drain and rinse the pineapple with a little extra vinegar, shaking dry. Place the sugar and the rest of the vinegar in a large pan and bring to the boil, simmering for 10 minutes, then add the pineapple, juices and all the remaining ingredients. Stir well and simmer gently for at least 40 minutes until the relish is thick and smooth. Pot, seal and label.

Keep for 2 weeks before using. Store in a cool, dry place.

Spiced Pineapple Chunks using tinned fruit

Goes very well with cold meats.

MAKES 4 X 375G JARS

| 1kg tinned pineapple cubes |
| 500g soft brown sugar |
| 900ml white wine vinegar |
| 1½ tablespoons mustard seeds |
| 1 cinnamon stick |
| 5 whole cloves |
| 1 small teaspoon ground ginger |
| 4 x 375g sterilised jam jars (page 44) |

Drain the pineapple. Put all the ingredients except the pineapple into a pan and bring gently to the boil, stirring well. Simmer for 20 minutes. Strain and return to the pan. Add the pineapple to the syrup and cook over a low heat until thick and reduced to a jammy consistency. Leave to cool before potting. Seal and label when cold

Keep for at least 3 months before using. Store in a cool, dry place.

 **PLUMS** In a good year a harvest of plums can reach glut proportions, therefore there are many recipes available to accommodate this bounty. Economically it makes sense to use British fruit in season, so look out for Victoria, Monarch, Czar, Early Rivers and a wonderful range of plums, of which these are only a small selection, varying from golden orange through to scarlet, crimson, purple and blue black. Some are marvellous for jams and

FRUIT

jellies, others bound to be pickled and spiced or turned into chutney and sauce. We do not often find the mysterious Quetsche-type plums, sharp and dark, which make superb sweet-sour pickles in this country, nor do we find the tiny scented golden Mirabelle, which makes a delicious apricoty conserve, but we do have the most glorious mixed bundle from gardens and allotments with which to make the most.

Several small items of interest to store away. Plums can be difficult to cook, some may require little water and constant watching, whilst another variety may turn out be very accommodating. Very ripe, overripe or bruised fruit just will not do in a preserve unless the recipe specifies otherwise. Overripe fruit lacks pectin and the quantity of sugar should be reduced accordingly, usually by 100g per kg of fruit, whilst overripe or bruised fruit will cause the jam to ferment on keeping. I have given a recipe for plum jam with pectin and before everyone shrieks that plums do not need the encouragement of commercial pectin, I would say in my defence that I do not find plums to be the super setters that they are cracked up to be. In fact, I think that they can be downright temperamental and I believe that this is caused by several factors. A wet, sunless summer will cause the fruit to become plump and succulent without allowing sugar and pectin to build up – very deceptive. Or during a hot summer, the fruit ripens very rapidly and has practically fallen from the tree before picking commences and overripe fruit does not give a satisfactory set. If you prefer to cook your plums without first stoning them, you will find that it gives a better flavour and set, although it causes inconvenience at the tea table, which is why stones should be tied into a muslin bag. If you leave fruit whole, try to slit or prick them and endeavour to catch the stones as they rise to the surface (a knob of unsalted butter stirred in at the end of cooking should facilitate this). The kernels added to the jam will give a slightly almondy taste, which will raise the jam to new heights.

In order to avoid gastronomic mistakes, the French for 'plum' is 'prune'.

Victoria Plum Conserve

MAKES 5 X 375G JARS

1kg Victoria plums

1.4kg white granulated sugar, warmed (page 17)

juice from 2 lemons

125ml commercial pectin

5 x 375g sterilised jam jars (page 44)

Wash the plums and slit them. Put them in a large pan with 150ml water, cover and simmer gently for roughly 20 minutes until they are soft without disintegrating. At this point, start retrieving the stones where you can. Add the warmed sugar with the lemon juice, stirring well until the sugar has dissolved. Bring to a full rolling boil for 3 minutes, stirring occasionally without being burned by erupting jam. Remove from the heat and stir in the pectin. Skim and stir for 2 minutes. Allow to cool before potting. Seal and label when cold.

This preserve can be eaten the next day. Store in a cool, dry place.

Mixed Plum Jam

An inspired and very useful idea for using up odds and ends of plums from your or your friends' gardens. It is a lovely deep golden-red jam with yummy chunks of Victorias hidden in it.

MAKES 3 X 375G JARS

1kg red, gold and Victoria plums

juice from 2 lemons

1kg white granulated sugar, warmed (page 17)

3 x 375g sterilised jam jars (page 44)

Wash and stone the plums. Victorias may be cut in half if large. Put the red and gold plums into a pan with a very small amount of water to prevent sticking, cover with a lid and simmer very carefully until soft. If the plums are very hard, you may need to add a little more warm water as you go along, but no more than 150ml in all. Add the Victorias and the lemon juice, then continue to cook, uncovered, until tender. Add the warmed sugar, stirring constantly until it has dissolved, then bring to the boil and boil hard until a set is obtained (see page 36). Pot, seal and label. This can be eaten the next day. Store in a cool, dry place.

FRUIT

Plum and Walnut Conserve

Two tablespoons of brandy or sherry stirred in with the nuts will give an extra richness.

MAKES 6 X 375G JARS

1kg red or golden plums

2 large thin-skinned sweet oranges

1 small lemon

25g each seedless raisins and currants

675g white granulated sugar

25g unsalted butter

100g walnuts

6 x 375g sterilised jam jars (page 44)

Wash, halve and stone the plums. Wash the oranges and lemon, chop the flesh and peel, discarding the pips, and put with the raisins and currants, either through a coarse mincer or the chop-chop machine. Put all the ingredients except the nuts into a pan and bring gently to the boil, stirring well until the sugar has dissolved. Reduce the heat and simmer until the jam is thick and a glossy set is obtained (see page 36). Chop the walnuts and stir them into the marmalade. Leave to cool before potting. Seal and label when cold.

This preserve can be eaten the next day. Store in a cool, dry place.

Tangy Plum Relish

MAKES 4 X 375G JARS

1kg plums

2 red onions

2 garlic cloves

25g fresh ginger

1 small fresh red chilli

1 orange

1 lemon

250g raisins

50g mixed glacé peel

450ml malt vinegar

15g pickling spice

450g soft brown sugar

4 x 375g sterilised jam jars (page 44)

Wash and stone the plums. Peel and chop the onions, garlic and ginger. Shred the chilli. Grate the zest from the orange and lemon and extract the juice. Chop the raisins and finely chop the glacé peel. Put all these ingredients into a pan with a very small amount of water, cover and cook gently for about 40 minutes. In the meantime, boil the vinegar with the pickling spice for 10 minutes, then cover and leave to cool.

When the plum mixture is cooked, strain the vinegar and add it to the pan. Heat through until the relish starts to bubble, then add the sugar, stirring continuously until it has dissolved. Bring to the boil and continue to boil until it is thick and soft. Pot, seal and label.

Keep for at least 2 weeks before using. Store in a cool, dry place.

Spicy Fruit Sauce

An absolutely delicious tangy and fruity sauce.

MAKES 5 X 600ML BOTTLES

1.75kg ripe plums

1 large onion

4 plump garlic cloves

50g fresh ginger

150g ripe tomatoes

100g raisins

1 teaspoon ground allspice

1 tablespoon ground coriander

1 teaspoon cayenne pepper

50g sea salt

1.15 litres malt vinegar

1 teaspoon fresh grated nutmeg

1 tablespoon turmeric

250g soft brown sugar

funnel

5 x 600ml sterilised bottles (page 44)

Wash and stone the plums; peel and chop the onion and garlic; peel and chop the ginger; wash the tomatoes. Put these ingredients together with the raisins, allspice, coriander, cayenne and salt into a large heavy-based pan with half the vinegar.

Bring gently to the boil, stirring well, and then reduce the heat and cover. Keep a very beady eye on the mixture, giving it an occasional vigorous stir to prevent the mixture catching on the bottom. Simmer for at least 1 hour until very soft and then liquidise. Return the purée to the pan with the remaining vinegar, spices and sugar. Cook gently, taking care that it does not burn, until the mixture is thick but pourable. This should take approximately 30–40 minutes. Using a funnel, bottle the sauce, seal tightly and label.

Keep for 2 months before using. Store in a cool, dry place.

Spiced Plums

Although this is a terrible tarradiddle, it really is a superb recipe and worth making. Try to use large Victoria plums and resist broaching for 6 weeks. Apricots, peaches, nectarines and greengages are all very delicious when given the same treatment.

MAKES 4 X 500G JARS

2kg slightly underripe plums

2kg white granulated sugar

900ml red wine vinegar

5–6cm piece of cinnamon stick

1 dessertspoon whole cloves

4 x 500g sterilised preserving jars

(page 44)

Wash the plums and prick them with a needle. Boil the sugar and vinegar together with the spices in a large pan and boil for several minutes. Put the plums into the syrup and bring it back to the boil, then remove the plums with a slotted spoon and place them in a large china bowl. Boil the syrup for another 5 minutes, skim and pour the syrup over the plums. Cover and leave for 24 hours.

Strain off the syrup once again, bring it to the boil and add the plums. Boil them for a further ½ minute and again transfer them to the bowl. Reboil the syrup for another 5 minutes and pour it back over the plums. Pot into the jars, cover with the syrup, seal tightly and label.

Keep for 3 months before using. Store in a cool, dry place.

PRUNES

We all know that the prune is a dried plum and for any reader who has, as a child, been institutionalised in hospital or school, the thought will send a frisson of fear down the spine because well-meaning adults have, at some time or another, insisted that said child should eat and enjoy. Prunes are far more suited to adult palates and they do make some very fine pickles, with or without the help of alcohol. To resuscitate prunes, soak them in cold water, tea (preferably Earl Grey) or brandy, depending on how flush you may be.

Spiced Prunes

MAKES 3 X 500ML JARS

500g fat, good-quality prunes with stones

strong cold tea

900ml malt vinegar

1 teaspoon whole cloves

a small piece of cinnamon stick

¼ teaspoon each fresh ground allspice and fresh grated nutmeg

1 blade mace

1 bay leaf

500g white granulated or soft
brown sugar

1 orange

3 x 500ml sterilised Kilner jars (page 44)

Put the prunes into a deep bowl and
cover with the tea (Indian is perfectly
acceptable, but it does not leave that
indefinable smoky perfume of some
China teas). Cover and leave overnight.

The next day, transfer the contents
of the bowl to a large pan and simmer
until just soft. Drain well, retaining 600ml
of the cooling liquid, and place this in a
pan with the vinegar, spices, bay leaf,
sugar and the thinly pared rind of the
orange. Bring to the boil, stirring well
until the sugar has dissolved. Boil for 5
minutes. Pack the prunes into the jars
and cover with the hot syrup – strained
or otherwise depending upon how
spicy you require the pickle to be. Seal
and label when cold.

Keep for at least 2 months before
using. Store in a cool, dry place.

Sherried Prunes

**Prunes and sherry combine remark-
ably well to make a rich and pleasant
dessert fruit.**

1kg good-quality prunes

1 lemon

1kg white granulated sugar

1 teaspoon vanilla extract

2 whole cloves

1 bottle of sherry – the very best is not
essential

8 x 500ml sterilised Kilner jars (page 44)

Put the prunes in a deep bowl
and cover with cold water. Leave
overnight. The next day, drain well.
Take 4 slices from the lemon and put
this with 1.5 litres water, the sugar,
vanilla extract and cloves, stir well,
bring to the boil and then simmer
for 15 minutes. Add the prunes and
continue to simmer for a further 30
minutes or until they are just tender
and, if necessary, you may need to
add a little more warm water. Remove
the prunes with a slotted spoon and
pack into the jars, leaving enough
room for the syrup and sherry. Half-fill
each jar with sherry and then add the
strained syrup to cover completely.
Seal tightly and label.

Keep for 3 months before using.
Store in a cool, dry place.

FRUIT

La confiture de vieux garcon aux fruits sec

The literal translation of the title is 'The old boy's preserve of dried fruits'. What it does to the old chaps, I dread to think, although I have a very good idea. Perhaps I am maligning the poor old boys because I have to say that many trendy young women are now making wonderful presents with these kinds of dried fruits. For a quick version, take the dried fruit of your choice and pack them into preserving jars, but do not fill tightly as the fruit needs room to swell. Fill up with alcohol: brandy, Cognac or Calvados for apples, slivovitz or kirsch for prunes and figs, peaches or raisins soaked in marc or vodka. Top up with alcohol over a period of 3 days, then seal securely and keep for at least 3 weeks before using.

MAKES 2KG ALCOHOL-SOAKED FRUIT

200g caster sugar
350g best-quality prunes
225g large soft dried apricots
225g preserved or soft dried pears
200g Smyrna raisins
750ml brandy or vodka
2 x 1kg sterilised preserving jars (page 44)

Put the sugar and 150ml water into a small pan and bring gently to the boil until the sugar has dissolved. Boil rapidly until it has reduced to a thin syrup. Put the fruit into separate bowls and divide the syrup among them. Cover and leave overnight, when they should expand and become quite plump. Drain off any surplus syrup. You can, if you wish, cut the fruit into smaller pieces, but it is not really necessary.

Arrange the fruit in the jars, adding the syrup as you go. Cover with the alcohol, making sure that there are no air bubbles. Seal tightly and keep for a good 3 months before using, topping up over a period of 3 days. Store in a cool, dry place.

QUINCE One of my warmest childhood memories is that of the spicy-sweet, sharp smell of ripening quinces on the kitchen dresser, mingling with wood smoke and baking cakes, the last of the summer sun and the promise of good things to come. It therefore comes as no surprise to learn that this remarkable fruit is enjoying a rise in popularity. The fruit is something of a cross between an apple and pear, ripening from lemon-yellow to deep gold and rather irregularly shaped. It has an odd and unmistakable taste, which gives a unique flavour to savoury dishes.

A good quince should be picked when just ripening and allowed to mature indoors to prevent the cores becoming hard and woody or too soft, which spoils their use in preserving. They do, however, make the most remarkable preserves of unique colour and taste, but because the peels and core take up a large percentage of the fruit – 50g to each 450g – they are usually tied in a muslin bag and used in the preserve, both for the pectin extract and to add colour.

Quinces are very high in pectin and the best basic proportions for quince preserves are 600ml water to 1.25kg sugar, and the juice of 1 lemon to each 1kg of fruit, plus the cores and peelings in a muslin bag unless the recipe states otherwise. If the fruit is very hard, it will absorb a deal of water. If this is so, then add a little more warm water. A last word on the estimable quince – do not store in close proximity to other foods as the scent is all pervading, and do not try to eat it raw for it is not agreeable.

FRUIT

Quince and Gooseberry Preserve

A smashing cheating recipe for those times when you have managed to buy glorious perfumed quinces and no other fruits remain. A really super flavour, astringently quince with the sharp, sweet bite of gooseberries.

MAKES 4 X 450G JARS

1kg quinces

350g tin gooseberries

850g white granulated sugar, warmed (page 17)

small muslin bag for pips and cores

4 x 450g sterilised jam jars (page 44)

Wash, peel and grate the quinces, tying the pips and cores into a muslin bag. Drain the juice from the tin of gooseberries, make it up to 300ml with water and put this into a pan with the grated quince and muslin bag. Cover and cook for about 1 hour until very soft, adding a little more warm water if it shows signs of drying out. Add the gooseberries and cook for a further 5 minutes. Remove the muslin bag, giving it a good squeeze. Add the warmed sugar and bring gently to the boil, stirring constantly until the sugar has dissolved. Boil hard until the quince becomes translucent and the syrup thick. Pot, seal and label.

This preserve can be eaten the next day or when cold.

Quince and Parsnip Preserve

An amazing preserve with an exceptional flavour.

MAKES 5 X 375G JARS

1kg quinces

1kg parsnips

1 large sweet orange and lemon

1kg white granulated sugar, warmed (page 17)

5 x 375g sterilised jam jars (page 44)

Peel and core the quinces and drop them into a bowl of lemony water to prevent discolouration. Wash and chop the parsnips. Slice the orange and lemon finely and put them into a pan with the parsnips and 1 litre water, cover and simmer for at least 1 hour until soft and limp looking. Turn the mixture into a large fine sieve and press gently to extract the maximum amount of juice with no pulp. Collect the juice and return it to the pan. Drain, dry and grate the quinces and add them to the juice, bring slowly to the boil and add the warmed sugar, stirring constantly until it has dissolved. Reduce the heat and simmer gently until the fruit is quite soft and the preserve has taken on a glazed translucent look. Pot, seal and label.

This preserve can be eaten the next day or when cold.

Quince Jelly

A fiery gold jelly that is as marvellous with cold meats and savoury pies as it is on hot toast. If you wish to give a slightly different flavour, a sprig of rosemary can be added to the first cooking.

MAKES 3 X 375G JARS

1kg quinces

white granulated sugar, warmed (page 17)

juice of 1 lemon

muslin or jelly bag

3 x 375g sterilised jam jars (page 44)

Wash and cut the quinces into smallish chunks. Put into a pan with 1 litre water, cover and cook for 1–2 hours until very

soft, adding a little more warm water if it seems to lack moisture. Turn the cooked fruit into a muslin or jelly bag and leave to drain overnight into a china bowl.

The next day, measure the juice gained and for each 600ml, take 450g warmed sugar. Return the juice to the clean pan with the lemon juice and heat gently, add the sugar and bring slowly to the boil, stirring continuously, until it has dissolved. Boil rapidly until a set is obtained (see page 36). Pot, seal and label.

This preserve can be eaten the next day or when cold.

Pâté de Coings or Cotignac

This is my sister's recipe, which I await every year as a Christmas treat from France. Like all quince goodies, they are awfully good for you.

MAKES 1–2 TRAYS OF LOZENGES

3kg quinces

1kg white granulated sugar, warmed (page 17)

small muslin bag for peels and cores

1 or 2 large flat baking tins – Swiss roll tins are ideal

Peel and core the quinces and cut
them into quarters. Tie the peels and
cores into a muslin bag and put this
into a large pan with the quinces and a
very little water. Cook over a low heat
until the quinces have become so soft
that they are a paste. You will have to
keep a very stern eye on the mixture
to prevent it burning. Remove the
muslin bag. Pass the quince through a
sieve or blender to give a good purée.

Transfer this to a scrupulously clean
pan and bring gently to bubbling, then
add the warmed sugar, stirring well
until it has dissolved. Continue to boil
gently, stirring and beating both to
ensure smoothness and avoid burning,
until the mixture is moisture free and
starts to leave the sides of the pan.

Spread the purée out to the depth
of a fruit pastille on the baking tins.
Preheat the oven to its lowest setting,
pop in the tin and leave the door ajar.
It should take about 10 hours for the
paste to dry out. When it is set, but
before it becomes quite cold, cut it into
lozenges and sprinkle with white sugar.

This preserve can be eaten when
cold and quite dried out. Keep in an
airtight tin lined with baking parchment.

RASPBERRY

The raspberry, which
is closely related to
the blackberry, is another fruit
that although well known to
gardeners, grows very frequently
in the wild. The fruit, made up
of soft one seeded druplets, is
carried on canes and is usually
red, although occasionally golden.
The soft, sweet-acid berries come
to fruition in midsummer and
although they make excellent
preserves with an adequate
amount of pectin, they are at their
very best when eaten fresh. When
picking raspberries, leave the
hull and stalk on the stem – in this
way you can be sure that they are
ripe for if they are not, they will
not slip easily from the cane. Do
not wash raspberries. If you fear
the presence of wriggly things
inside, do not be tempted to soak
them out, just lay the fruit flat on a
dish and leave it in a cool place,
where hopefully the tiny maggots
will leave home (if you put it in the
fridge, then cover with clingfilm).
Although a wet summer can cause

raspberries to retain too much water, which may eventually cause a mould to form on the jam through no apparent fault of your own, it is fair to say that the usual cause of mould in the preserve is the use of squishily overripe fruit. This not only looks unpleasant, but causes the preserve to become 'winey'.

Raspberry Jam

A good, quick soft-set recipe, ensuring whole fruit and a deliciously fresh flavour. If you prefer a seedless jam, then pass the fruit and juices through a fine sieve before adding the sugar. A standard recipe for loganberries and blackberries as well as raspberries.

MAKES 4 X 375G JARS

1kg raspberries

1kg white granulated sugar, warmed (page 17)

4 x 375g sterilised jam jars (page 44)

Pick over the fruit, removing stalks and insects if necessary. Put the fruit into a pan and slowly bring the heat up until the juices are starting to run and the fruit softened. Cook gently for 2 minutes, then add the warmed sugar, stirring well until it has dissolved. Allow it to come to the boil, still stirring well, and then remove from the heat. Pot, then seal and label when cold.

This preserve can be eaten the next day or when cold.

Three Fruit Summer Jam

This preserve can be made with the addition of blackcurrants, but I think that they mask the flavour of the finer fruit.

MAKES 5 X 375G JARS

500g raspberries

500g strawberries

500g redcurrants

1.5kg white granulated sugar, warmed (page 17)

5 x 375g sterilised jam jars (page 44)

Pick over the raspberries and strawberries. Wash the redcurrants, removing from the stalks through the tines of a fork. Put the redcurrants into a pan and heat gently until their juice starts to flow. Add the strawberries and allow them to soften, then pop in the raspberries, bring to boiling point and add the warmed sugar, stirring carefully until it has dissolved.

Bring to the boil again and boil rapidly until a set is obtained (see page 36). Because the redcurrants contain a boost of pectin, this should not take more than 5 minutes, thus ensuring that the flavour stays fresh. Allow to cool a little before potting. Seal and label when cold.

This preserve can be eaten the next day or when cold.

Raspberry and Apple Jelly

This is a very good way to use up small or unripe berries and windfall apples. Gooseberries may be substituted for the apples; most of the soft fruit for the raspberries. Nice set and a super taste.

MAKES 4 X 375G JARS

1kg raspberries

500g cooking apples

white granulated sugar, warmed (page 17)

muslin or jelly bag

4 x 375g sterilised jam jars (page 44)

Pick over the raspberries. Wash and chop the apples and place both fruit into a pan with 450ml water. Cook for about 30 minutes until very soft, then turn into a muslin or jelly bag and leave to drain overnight into a bowl without any helpful poking and prodding.

The next day, measure the juice gained and for each 600ml, take 450g warmed sugar. Return the juice to the pan, heat gently and add the sugar, stirring well until it has dissolved. Bring to the boil and boil hard until a set is obtained (see page 36). Pot, seal and label.

This preserve can be eaten the next day or when cold.

Raspberry Preserve

Another excellent method for making blackberry or loganberry preserve too.

MAKES 4 X 375G JARS

1kg raspberries

1kg white caster sugar

¼ teaspoon vanilla extract

4 x 375g sterilised jam jars (page 44)

Pick over the raspberries and put into a large china bowl with the sugar. Cover and leave for at least 12 hours.

The next day, turn the contents of the bowl into a pan and add 4 tablespoons of water, bring to the boil, stirring gently, and then boil for 7 minutes. Remove the fruit with a slotted spoon and lay in a sieve, transferring any juices that drip through to the pan. Continue to boil the syrup until it is very thick and drops very slowly from a spoon. Add the raspberries and a few drops of vanilla extract. Remove from the heat and cool before potting. Seal and label when cold. This can be eaten the next day or when cold.

Tutti Frutti

Prepare a stone jar with a tight lid, making sure that it is not porous. Begin the season with 500g small, firm strawberries. Lay them in the jar and cover with 500g white caster sugar. Add brandy to cover. Carefully tie down with double paper tied with string. When the raspberries come into season, open the lid carefully, stir well to move the sugar at the bottom and repeat the process with 500g raspberries and 500g sugar. Once again, cover with brandy and tie down. Repeat the process with stoned cherries, sugar and brandy in the same amounts. Tie down and use at Christmas, although this alcoholic lovely will keep for ages. 1 litre bottle of brandy, of moderate quality, should accommodate at least 2kg fruit. The recommended method of enjoying this treat is to serve by the half-filled wine glass, accompanied by sponge fingers!

Raspberry Wine or Ratafia

An exquisite wine, which can be diluted with sugar syrup and soda or mineral water.

MAKES 2 X 600ML BOTTLES

1kg raspberries

900ml good red wine without chemicals

white granulated sugar

½ lemon

2 x 600ml sterilised bottles with corks (page 44)

Hull and clean the raspberries without washing them, lay them out in a shallow dish and cover them with the wine. Spread a muslin cloth over the top to prevent the odd fly from drowning itself in drunken glory. Leave for 48 hours, stirring occasionally with a wooden spoon.

Turn the whole lot into a clean muslin cloth and gently press out every drop of juice. Measure the liquid gained and for each 600ml, take 450g sugar and put both into a stainless-steel or enamel pan with juice from the lemon and bring gently to the boil. When the sugar has dissolved, boil for 5 minutes, remove from the heat and leave to get cold. Bottle, seal with corks, label and keep for 15 days in a cool, dry place before broaching.

RHUBARB

Rhubarb can lurk, without interference, in an odd spot in the garden, throwing out delicious red and green stems and architectural leaves for years. If it is boosted with slavish applications of manure and mulch, it will reward you accordingly and you may pull the stalks throughout the summer to make some of the best British puds. An important fact to know about rhubarb is that the leaves and the bulb-type end of stem are poisonous and must be discarded. Rhubarb has a high oxalic acid content, as do spinach and sorrel, which is why they set your teeth on edge. Never cook rhubarb in aluminium as the acid reacts against it. Rhubarb in preserve making is economical, but not always very accommodating for the pectin content is fairly low and consequently it should be cooked without water to achieve a set. Early rhubarb will need a little water to soften it and will set better, but late rhubarb will need no water and requires the addition of lemon to bring about a set. Nevertheless, it is one of those fruit, like plums, which cannot be 100 per cent guaranteed to co-operate, unless used with apple, blackcurrant, lemon or gooseberry.

Here is a very handy tip, which may well cause roars of rage amongst the purists, but it is an economical godsend for rhubarb jam that refuses to set: add it to chutney, particularly apple or marrow. For each 1kg main fruit used in the chutney recipe, take 675g jam, reduce the sugar by at least half according to taste, and add the jam when the sugar is added, stirring well to ensure that it is completely mixed. The same method can be applied to plum jam, which also gives problems. Some chutneys are much improved by this deception.

FRUIT

Rhubarb and Angelica Conserve

For a rhubarb and ginger preserve, you can substitute the 50g angelica for 25g candied peel and 25g crystallised ginger to make a more perfumed preserve.

MAKES 5 X 375G JARS

1kg rhubarb stems

2 large cooking apples

225g fat raisins

800g white granulated sugar

2 lemons

50g angelica

5 x 375g sterilised jam jars (page 44)

Wash and cut up the rhubarb. Wash, peel, core and slice the apples and chop the raisins. Turn the fruit into a china bowl with the sugar, cover and leave overnight.

The next day, grate the rind from the lemons and extract the juice. Chop the angelica. Transfer the contents of the bowl to a stainless-steel pan (not aluminium) and add the angelica, lemon rind and juice. Bring gently to the boil, stirring well, and then boil rapidly until a set is obtained (see page 36). Pot, seal and label.

This preserve can be eaten the next day or when cold.

Rhubarb and Lemon Marmalade

Sharp, bitter citrus marmalade for a palate cleansing breakfast experience! A similar recipe can be made by substituting oranges for the lemons, but it is a sweeter, lighter, more jammy preserve.

MAKES 6 X 375G JARS

4 large thin-skinned lemons

1kg rhubarb stems

1kg white granulated sugar, warmed (page 17)

small muslin bag for pips

6 x 375g sterilised jam jars (page 44)

Wash the lemons and, working on a plate to collect the juices, finely shred or mince the fruit, extracting all the juice and tying the pips into a muslin bag. Put the fruit, juice and pips into a large bowl with 450ml water, cover and leave to stand overnight to allow the peel to soften.

The next day, wash, trim and cut the

rhubarb into pieces. Turn the contents of the bowl into a stainless-steel pan with the rhubarb, stir well and simmer for 20 minutes. Remove the muslin bag, giving it a good squeeze, and add the warmed sugar, stirring well until it has dissolved. Bring to the boil and boil hard until a set is obtained (see page 36). Pot, seal and label.

This preserve can be eaten the next day or when cold.

Rhubarb and Beetroot Chutney

Mild, soft and sweet and a very useful way of using up rhubarb and beet-root from the garden that are slightly past their best.

MAKES 6 X 375G JARS

1kg rhubarb stems

225g onions

2 garlic cloves

450g freshly cooked beetroot

200g fat raisins

450ml malt vinegar

2 teaspoons sea salt

225g soft brown sugar

6 x 375g sterilised jam jars (page 44)

Wash, string and chop the rhubarb stems and place them in a stainless-steel pan with hardly enough water to cover. Simmer until barely soft, which should not take long. Strain and do not discard the juice. Peel the onions and garlic, chop finely and place in the pan with just enough of the rhubarb juice to cover and simmer for about 15 minutes until soft. Peel and chop the beetroot into dice and add it to the pan with the rhubarb, raisins and vinegar and continue to cook gently until the mixture is thick. Add the salt and sugar, stirring well until the sugar is dissolved, then bring to a gentle boil, stirring occasionally to ensure that the chutney does not burn. After about an hour, when the mixture is thick with little excess moisture, stir well and pot, seal and label.

Keep for 1 month before using. Store in a cool, dry place.

Hot Rhubarb Chutney

A sharp, hot chutney with a tangy taste.

MAKES 5 X 375G JARS

1kg rhubarb stems

250g onions

4 garlic cloves

2 thin-skinned lemons

1 hot green chilli (as long or as small as
you like)
450ml white wine or cider vinegar
225g sultanas
2 teaspoons sea salt
350g golden granulated sugar
5 x 375g sterilised jam jars (page 44)

Wash, string and chop the rhubarb
stems and place them in a stainless-steel
pan. Peel and roughly chop the onions
and garlic. Wash and chop the lemons,
removing the pips as you go. Chop
the chilli (if you prefer to use a ready-
prepared 'lazy chilli' then 1–2 teaspoons
will suffice). Put the onions, garlic,
lemons and chilli into a blender with
the vinegar and zizz until it is all well
chopped, adding the sultanas and giving
them a brief whirl just to cut the fruit.
Put all these ingredients into the pan
with the rhubarb, add the salt and cook
gently for about 40 minutes until soft
and nicely amalgamated. Add the sugar,
stirring well until it has dissolved, and
bring slowly to the boil, continuing to stir
to prevent burning. Simmer for a further
40 minutes until the mixture has become
thick. Stir well. Pot, seal and label.

This chutney benefits from keeping
at least 1 month in a cool, dark place
before broaching.

SLOE

Blackthorn is the
true wild plum
of Europe. Small,
dense, spiny and dark,
the flowers that appear
before the leaves are frosty white,
glittering amongst the lethal
thorns and turning to a purple-
black plum-like fruit, which will
eventually have a soft white
bloom. The acid flesh is green
and if bitten into will cause teeth,
tongue and tonsils to shrivel with
shock. However unpalatable
the fruit may be, it makes a
very drinkable gin and several
interesting preserves. Many years
ago the fruit was roasted and
eaten as it was – tough times. It is
best to pick the fruit after the first
frost, but most people pick them
before then, otherwise the birds
will have had them.

Sloe and Apple Jelly

Delicious with mutton, hare and
rabbit.

**MAKES 4 X 375G JARS OR MORE
SMALL JARS**

1kg sloes

350g cooking or crab apples
white granulated sugar, warmed (page 17)
muslin or jelly bag
4 x 375g sterilised jam jars or more
small jars (page 44)

Wash and prick the sloes, unless they
have been picked after the first frost.
Wash and chop the apples and put both
fruit into a pan with just enough water to
cover. Simmer until very soft, turn into
a muslin or jelly bag and leave to drain
overnight into a china bowl.

The next day, measure the juice
gained and for each 600ml gained, take
675g warmed sugar. Return the juice to
the pan, heat gently and add the sugar,
stirring well until it has dissolved. Bring
to the boil and boil hard until a set is
obtained (see page 36). Pot, seal
and label.

This preserve can be eaten the next
day or when cold.

Sloe Gin

Damson gin or mulberry gin, which
is absolutely gorgeous, may be made
in the same way, but there is no need
to prick the latter. Sloes and damsons
may also be transformed in the same
way with a bottle of vodka. Spiced
sloe gin can easily be made by infiltrating one thinly sliced, thin-skinned
lemon, 1 piece each of bruised dried
root ginger and cinnamon stick and
1 teaspoon whole cloves into the
layered, sugared sloes before drowning them in gin. Purist that I am, I
prefer the original recipe.

MAKES 1 TALL JAR
a quantity of fat, black sloes
white granulated sugar
1 bottle of gin
a tall sterilised jar, preferably a
preserving jar (page 44)

Wash the sloes thoroughly and prick
them through with a needle to release
the juices. Put enough sloes in the jar
to reach one third of the way up. If you
have a sweet tooth, add 4 tablespoons
of sugar, if you are a more aesthetic
drinker, 2 tablespoons will do. Pour in
the gin to cover.

Seal tightly and shake every day until
Christmas, or when passing. My bottle
gets hidden in a dark cupboard to avoid
it 'evaporating' when the family is home.
If you collect your sloes in October, the
macerating period should not be less
than 3 months.

FRUIT

STRAWBERRY

Strawberries, when they are cultivated lovingly and domestically, are the most delicious sweetly acid fruit imaginable. When they are grown in warm and sunny fields for local consumption on a small scale, they are equally good and a bonus for jam makers for you can usually pick your own at a reduced cost. However, grown for the polythene-packed, vast commercial market, bombarded with science, frozen and forced, they are too often tasteless, scarlet shells of awe-inspiring glossiness and uniform size filled with watery pap.

Cultivated strawberries make delicious preserves and jams from the simple to the highly complex. Despite all the recipes and ideas put forward to obtain a good set, strawberries are so low in pectin that this is virtually impossible, even with the aid of lemon juice. The most that one can hope for is a gorgeous goo, which will spread well and taste authentic. Strawberries need no water for cooking unless specified and will reduce considerably during cooking, giving an uneconomical result, but preferable I feel to the bright, super-sweet commercial product. Using a juice from a high pectin fruit, using a specific jam making or preserving sugar or resorting to the very helpful commercial pectin will save many shredded nerves.

Strawberry Jam with Commercial Pectin

This is the only way to ensure a well set jam with whole fruit, fresh flavour and good colour, therefore I make no apology for using commercial pectin.

MAKES 6 X 375G JARS

1kg small, dark strawberries

2 lemons

1.25g white granulated sugar

small knob of unsalted butter

125ml commercial pectin

6 x 375g sterilised jam jars (page 44)

FRUIT

Clean and hull the strawberries. Extract 3 tablespoons of juice from the lemons and put the strawberries, lemon juice and sugar into a large saucepan. Leave for 1 hour, stirring occasionally. Heat gently, stirring constantly, until the sugar has dissolved.

Add the butter and bring to a full rolling boil for 4 minutes, stirring a little to prevent sticking. Remove from the heat and stir in the pectin. Skim and stir for 2 minutes. Leave to cool for 15 minutes and stir well before potting. Seal and label when cold.

This preserve can be eaten the next day or when cold.

Whole Strawberry Jam

A very good recipe, especially for the smaller strawberries. A special conserve can be made using this recipe by adding a good slug of kirsch – about 1 tablespoon can be added to the syrup before it is poured over the strawberries.

MAKES 3 X 375G JARS

1kg small, sharp strawberries

1kg white granulated sugar

a few drops of vanilla extract

3 x 375g sterilised jam jars (page 44)

Clean and hull the strawberries and put them into a china bowl with the sugar. Cover and leave for 12 hours.

The next day, transfer the fruit and sugar to a pan, add 2 tablespoons water and heat gently, shaking and stirring with a wooden spoon, but not breaking the strawberries. As soon as the fruit sinks to the bottom of the pan, which means it is soft and takes approximately 10–15 minutes, lift them out with a slotted spoon and pack into the warm jars. Add the vanilla extract to the syrup and simmer until it is thick enough to coat the back of a spoon. Stir well and pour over the fruit to cover. Seal and label when cold.

This preserve can be eaten the next day or when cold.

Strawberry conserve

Not only does the addition of high pectin redcurrant juice provide a necessary setting quality, but also lends a much sharper, astounding flavour.

MAKES 4 X 375G JARS

1kg strawberries

1kg white granulated sugar

300ml redcurrant juice

4 x 375g sterilised jam jars (page 44)

Clean and hull the strawberries. Put them into a pan with the sugar and heat gently, stirring with care until the sugar has dissolved and the strawberries are soft but not disintegrating. Add the warmed redcurrant juice and bring to the boil. Boil gently until a set is

obtained (see page 36). Allow to cool for about 15 minutes and stir well to distribute the strawberries evenly. Pot, seal and label when quite cold.

This preserve can be eaten the next day or when cold.

Strawberries in Madeira

Quite delicious and silly-making strawberries for a grand dessert.

MAKES 2 X 500G JARS

1kg ripe strawberries

225g caster sugar

Madeira or sweet sherry

2 x 500g wide-necked sterilised preserving jars (page 44)

Make sure that your strawberries are pristine and perfect. Clean and hull them and pack them into the jars in layers with the sugar, filling up to the top. Pour in the liquor of choice until the fruit is covered, doing this slowly to ensure that there are no air bubbles. Seal tightly, label and store in a cool dry place.

Keep for 1 month until they become quite sozzled before using.

FRUIT

FENNEL

Fennel is one of those delightfully feathery herbs, which is very decorative in the garden. Not dissimilar to dill, it is a lovely soft bright green or a deep bronze, having a mass of umbrella clusters of frothy yellow flowers that, in hotter countries, smother the roadsides in the spring. The stems and seeds have a strong and aromatic taste of aniseed. Used particularly for cooking fish and on barbecues to give a smoky hint of the fresh herbs.

Gooseberry and Fennel Jelly

A very good savoury jelly that goes well with any cold fish dish and particularly freshly cooked mackerel. As gooseberry is such a brilliant fruit to use in making herb jellies, experiment with some of your favourites, using flower petals as well as herbs: marigolds for a tangy taste, rose for perfume and dandelion for a severe and unexpectedly nice jolt to the taste buds.

MAKES 8 X 175G JARS

1kg green gooseberries

a handful of fresh fennel stalks

white granulated sugar, warmed (page 17)

several heads of fennel seeds

muslin or jelly bag

8 x 175g sterilised jam jars (page 44)

Wash the gooseberries and put them into a pan with 300ml water. Wash and chop the fennel stalks and add these to the pan, then cover and simmer gently, giving an occasional mashing, until the fruit is very soft. Turn into a muslin or jelly bag and leave to drain overnight into a bowl.

The next day, measure the juice and for every 600ml juice, take 450g warmed sugar. Return the juice to the pan, heat gently and add the sugar, stirring well until it has dissolved. Bring to the boil and boil hard until a set is obtained (see page 36). Meanwhile, clean and dry the seed heads well. When the jelly is ready, skim it and remove from the heat. Allow to cool a little and half-fill each jar. Place a piece of the fennel head in each one and fill up with the jelly. Seal and label when cold.

This preserve can be eaten the next day or when cold. It is best kept in the fridge once opened.

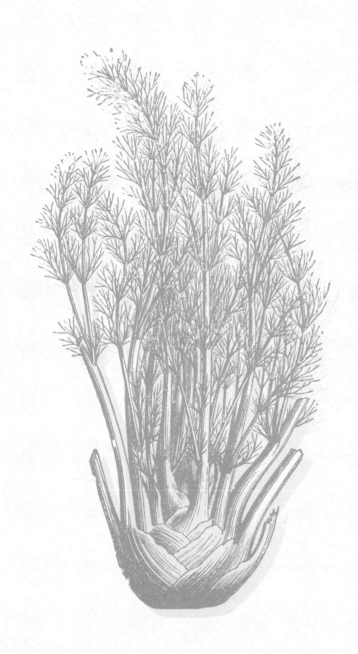

HERBS

MINT

Although there are more than 40 varieties of mint, we usually only come into contact with the most familiar lamb's mint or green-pea mint, better known as spearmint. Yet there is also applemint, eau de cologne, pineapple, peppermint, ginger, orange and lemon and of course the wild mints – pennyroyal, wild water, calamint – to name just a fantastically fragrant few. Although we are very familiar with mint sauce, mint is also delicious when stirred into a savoury apple or gooseberry jelly, whilst the more unusual mints make delicate fruit jellies based on crab apple, gooseberry, red and white currants. In the Middle East, mint sauce is turned into an ice-cold refreshing sherbet. Not only invaluable in food, mint is an asset to a healthy regime – mint prevents flies in your house, catmint prevents fleas in your pets, fresh mint tea purifies a sluggish system and chopped mint in your food aids digestion.

There is nothing so refreshing as fresh mint crushed beneath your nose and inhaled deeply. Clears the fug away amazingly well.

A few handy hints for making the much beloved mint sauce. A little hot water poured onto the chopped mint leaves will set the colour. Sugar should be dissolved in a tiny drop of hot water before adding to mint sauce. A swift and easy way to make mint sauce for immediate use is to put the whole lot into a liquidiser – mint, vinegar, sugar et al – the results are then achieved in one fell swoop. To take evasive action to ensure that you have a supply of mint sauce throughout the winter months, take 50g fresh young mint leaves and 150ml vinegar. Boil the vinegar and leave it to cool. Wash, dry and chop the mint finely, pack into a large jar and completely cover with the vinegar. To re-use, remove the quantity you require, sealing the jar tightly afterwards. Put into a small pot and add a little dissolved sugar. Add extra vinegar if necessary.

HERBS

Mint Sauce Jelly

This is a lovely jelly with lamb and has the added advantage over mint sauce that it does keep well. Can also be used for basting lamb.

MAKES 8 X 175G JARS

1kg cooking or crab apples
white malt vinegar
a very large handful of fresh garden mint
white granulated sugar, warmed (page 17)
muslin or jelly bag
8 x 175g sterilised jars (page 44)

Wash and chop the apples roughly, put them into a pan with just enough water to cover and simmer for about 1 hour until very soft. When cooked, turn into a muslin or jelly bag and leave to drip overnight.

The next day, measure the juice gained and for every 500ml, take 150ml vinegar. Wash and shake dry the mint and put it with the vinegar into a blender and zizz well. Add the minty vinegar to the apple juice, measure again, and for every 500ml take 450g warmed sugar. Return the juice to the pan and heat gently, add the sugar and stir until it has dissolved. Bring to the boil and boil rapidly until a set is obtained (see page 36). This will take a little longer than usual because of the addition of vinegar. Allow to cool a little before potting, and seal and label when cold.

This preserve can be eaten the next day or when cold. It is best kept in the fridge once opened.

NASTURTIUM

A bright display of cheerful nasturtiums in your garden will last right up to the first frosts, continuously producing their seed pods, which can be made up into false capers, hotter and spicier than the genuine article. The flowers and leaves also make a very unusual and tangy sauce. Pick the nasturtium seed just after the flower has withered, when they are still soft without any hard central core, and pick the flowers and leaves whilst they are still fresh and dry. It is essential that you use flowers, leaves and seeds that have not been afflicted with the beastly blackfly. Nasturtium leaves and flowers can be added to pickles, white vinegar and salads to give colour and taste.

HERBS

Pickled Nasturtium Pods

MAKES 6 X 175G JARS

fresh nasturtium seeds

600ml white malt or cider vinegar

1 level tablespoon sea salt

1 teaspoon black peppercorns

2 whole cloves

1 teaspoon whole allspice

6 x 175g sterilised jars (page 44)

Wash the seeds well and leave overnight in a brine made with 50g sea salt to 600ml water. This solution has the effect of softening the seeds and removing any bitterness. In the meantime, put the vinegar, salt and spices into a pan and bring to the boil, remove from the heat, cover and leave to become cold. Strain before using. Drain and pat the 'capers' dry, pack them closely into the jars, cover with the cold vinegar and seal tightly. Keep for at least 1 month in a cool, dry place before using.

This preserve is best kept in the fridge once opened.

Nasturtium Sauce

An unusual sauce with a hot peppery tang.

MAKES 6 X 175ML BOTTLES

225g nasturtium flowers and leaves

4 shallots

3 garlic cloves

600ml brown malt vinegar

½ teaspoon sea salt

½ teaspoon cayenne pepper

soy sauce

muslin cloth for straining

1 large sterilised heat-resistant jar and 6 x 175ml sterilised bottles (page 44)

Examine the leaves and petals carefully for insects before putting them into the jar. Peel and chop the shallots and garlic and place these in a pan with the vinegar, salt and cayenne pepper. Boil for 10 minutes and pour over the nasturtiums in the jar.

Cover tightly, shake well and leave for 2 months in a cool, dry place. Strain through a muslin cloth, stir in soy sauce to taste, pour into the bottles and label.

This sauce is best kept in the fridge once opened.

HERBS

ROSEMARY

The shrubby, evergreen rosemary is one of the most ancient of cottage garden herbs. From formal knot gardens to rambling beds of lilac and lupin, this pretty bush, with its dark green, silver-backed, spiky leaves and blue-lipped flowers, has perfumed the air of England on many hot summer days with its' pungent, aromatic scent, which can be captured throughout the year by popping a pretty flowered sprig into a jar of caster sugar. To my mind there is a traditional trinity of herbs: rosemary, sage and lavender, which heal and protect as well as give great value in the kitchen. Rosemary is for remembrance and some of the most discreet and useful ways of remembering are to make delightful sugars, vinegars and oils with it.

Hot Tomato and Rosemary Jelly

A very peppy and colourful jelly to go with cold meats.

MAKES 8 X 175G JARS

2 fresh red chillies

1 lemon

450g tin tomatoes

good sprigs of fresh rosemary

300ml red wine vinegar

¼ teaspoon sea salt

900g white granulated sugar, warmed (page 17)

1 x 250ml bottle of commercial pectin

muslin or jelly bag

8 x 175g sterilised jam jars (page 44)

Shred the chillies, grate the rind from the lemon and extract the juice, which should be kept until later. Put the tomatoes and their juice, chillies, lemon rind and a few of the rosemary sprigs into a large pan with 300ml water. Cover and cook gently for roughly 40 minutes until soft and disintegrated. Turn into a clean muslin or jelly bag and leave to drain until all the liquid is through, but do not be tempted to prod or squeeze out the juice, which will result in a cloudy jelly.

HERBS

Return the juice, lemon juice, vinegar and salt to the clean pan and heat gently, add the warmed sugar and stir continuously until it has dissolved. Bring to the boil and boil hard for 5 minutes.

Remove the saucepan from the heat and stir in the pectin, taking care that the jelly does not froth over. Stir for 2 minutes. Remove the scum from the top and leave to cool a little before half-filling each jar and adding a clean sprig of rosemary to each pot before filling to the top. Allow to become cold before sealing and labelling.

This preserve can be eaten the next day or when cold. It is best kept in the fridge once opened.

Rosemary Oil

Try this concoction with the leaves of marjoram, basil, sage, thyme or mint. Fennel will also give a lovely oil to use in mayonnaise – the method is the same. Well-pounded seed herbs such as coriander also make a very flavoursome oil.

MAKES 1 X 500ML BOTTLE

6 tablespoons crushed fresh rosemary leaves

600ml sunflower oil or very light olive oil

3 tablespoons white wine vinegar

1 x 1 litre sterilised preserving jar with a tight-fitting lid and 1 x 500ml sterilised bottle (page 44)

The best way to crush any herb is to put them into a liquidiser with either a little oil or vinegar and give them a quick zizz, otherwise it is down to the old elbow grease with the pestle and mortar or basin and blunt instrument. Turn them into the jar and add the oil and vinegar, leaving a good space at the top to shake.

Seal tightly and put on a warm windowsill to infuse gently. Shake every time you pass. Leave for 3 weeks and then strain the oil, crushing the herb on the sieve to ensure that you squeeze out every last drop of aromatic juice. Repeat the process with the same oil and fresh leaves if the oil is not strong enough. Pour into a clean bottle and add a fresh, clean sprig of rosemary. Seal tightly and label.

This preserve is best kept in the fridge once opened.

Rosemary and Crab Apple Jelly

This, to my mind, is the nicest of the herb jellies and is superb with lamb. If you like the smell of rosemary, then making this jelly will be a perfect pleasure. Having said that, this recipe works very well with other 'woody' herbs.

MAKES 8 X 175G JARS

1kg crab apples

large handful of fresh rosemary sprigs

white wine vinegar

white granulated sugar, warmed (page 17)

muslin or jelly bag

8 x 175g sterilised jars (page 44)

Wash and chop the apples up small. Place in a preserving pan and cover with water. Cook for about 1 hour until mushy and soft, adding more warm water if necessary. When soft, turn into a muslin or jelly bag and leave to drain overnight.

The next day, wash the rosemary, keeping back a few nice sprigs. Heat the apple juice gently in a covered pan, add the rosemary and simmer gently for 5 minutes. Remove from the heat, cover and leave to stand. When the house is filled with the pungent, aromatic smell of the rosemary, you should have a good infusion. More prosaically, allow about 20 minutes. Strain, measure this liquid and for every 600ml gained, take 150ml vinegar. Mix the liquids together and for every 600ml then obtained, take 450g warmed sugar. Reheat the liquid gently and add the warmed sugar, stirring well until it has dissolved. Bring to the boil and boil rapidly until a set is obtained (see page 36). This may take a little longer due to the addition of vinegar. Skim.

Wash and dry the remaining rosemary. When the jelly has cooled a little, half-fill the pots, placing a sprig of rosemary upright in each jar. The jelly should be set enough to support it. Fill to the top with the remaining jelly. Seal and label when cold.

This preserve can be eaten the next day or when cold. It is best kept in the fridge once opened.

HERBS

SAGE

There are over 500 species of sage, most of which have their uses in the kitchen or cure cupboard. The medicinal properties of this Mediterranean herb are far-reaching, the name alone, *Salvia*, means to heal and not only is it used as a great antiseptic, but it is a ward against colds, senility, failing memory, failing strength, counteracts shock and stress and prevents hair and teeth falling out. So how about that – and I forgot to mention that it is paramount in the kitchen, where it needs to be used with delicacy. Sage is wonderful with most rich meats as it subdues fatty elements. At one time it was a useful anti-sickness device if meat or fish was a tad dubious.

Sage and Cider Jelly

An absolutely delicious and unique flavour – superb with cold pork.

MAKES 8 X 175G JARS

50g dried sage

900g white granulated sugar

450ml sweet cider

1 x 250ml bottle of commercial pectin

8–10 fresh sage leaves

muslin for straining

8 x 175g sterilised jars (page 44)

Crumble the dried sage (do not use powdered sage) and put it in a small basin. Boil 150ml water and pour it over the sage. Cover and leave for 15 minutes. Strain through a muslin cloth. If necessary, add enough water to make up to 150ml liquid.

Put into a large saucepan and add the sugar and cider. Heat gently to boiling point, stirring well until the sugar has dissolved. Pour in the pectin, stirring constantly, and take care that the whole lot does not boil over. Boil for 1 minute. Skim and leave to stand for a minute or two.

Half-fill the jars with the cooling liquid. Make sure that you have a few pieces of prettily shaped, clean and dry sage leaves, place one in each jar and then fill up with the cooling jelly. Seal and label when cold. This can be eaten the next day or when cold. It is best kept in the fridge once opened.

Sage and Apple Preserve

Both apple and sage cut the richness of pork and are a traditional accompaniment – you can vary the amount of sage used to suit your taste. This recipe is utterly delicious and one that gives you the chance to get to grips with sterilising sauces (see pages 44–5).

MAKES 4–6 X 175G JARS

1kg cooking apples

1 small onion

100g caster sugar

1 teaspoon salt

1 teaspoon freshly ground pepper

2 good teaspoons dried sage

1 small teaspoon Worcester sauce

1 dessertspoon white malt vinegar

25g unsalted butter

4–6 x 175g sterilised preserving jars (page 44)

Wash the apples and chop them roughly. Peel and slice the onion. Put the apples and onion into a saucepan, add 4 tablespoons water, cover and simmer gently until the mixture is very soft. Stir in the remaining ingredients and continue to cook until well mixed. Pass through a sieve and return to the heat. Bring to the boil and pour into the jars. Continue as for sterilising sauces (see pages 44–5). This preserve can be eaten the next day or when cold. It is best kept in the fridge once opened.

TARRAGON

Tarragon appears to be quite rarely used as an 'everyday' herb and yet it combines well with tomatoes, garlic and pot vegetables, lends enchantment to chicken, eggs and creamy sauces and should always be added to a good fines herbes mixture. Omelettes, stuffings and marinades will all benefit from its distinctive, slightly aniseed taste and it is a very valuable herb to use in pickling, particularly pickled plums. Historically, tarragon has always enjoyed a fine reputation in herbal medicine, keeping the digestion and blood pure. The tarragon to grow or buy is French tarragon, not Russian, and it is worth knowing that if the herb is cooked too long in a dish, it may become bitter. Use tarragon jelly and vinegar to add that distinctive touch to sauces and savouries.

Tarragon Jelly

A nice sprig of tarragon can be added to each pot on cooling. 1 tablespoon of the freshly chopped herb can be stirred into the jelly before potting or 4 teaspoons of dried tarragon can be used instead of fresh. Sage may be treated in the same way.

MAKES 4 X 375G JARS

2 good sprigs of fresh tarragon

600ml apple or crab apple juice

2 tablespoons red wine vinegar

350g white granulated sugar, warmed (page 17)

4 x 375g sterilised jam jars (page 44)

Wash and dry the tarragon and put it into a pan with the apple juice and vinegar. Bring to the boil and boil gently for 10 minutes. Add the warmed sugar, stirring well until it has dissolved. Bring to the boil and boil hard for about 40 minutes until it is nicely wobbly, then pour through a sieve before it cools. Pot, seal and label.

This preserve can be eaten the next day or when cold. It is best kept in the fridge once opened.

Tarragon Vinegar

Tarragon vinegar is superb when added to sauces, especially those that are slightly piquant, and excellent in salad dressings. Many very delicious vinegars are made by this method – basil, sage, marjoram, thyme and the delicately aromatic lemon thyme – to name a few.

MAKES 1 X 600ML BOTTLE

50g fresh tarragon

600ml white wine or cider vinegar

a glass jar with non-metal lid and

1 x 600ml good sterilised bottle with a cork (page 44)

Pick the tarragon before it blooms and before the full sun has had time to draw out the aromatic oils. Wash, dry and strip the leaves from the stalks, pack into the jar and cover with the vinegar. Seal tightly and leave it to infuse on a warm windowsill for at least 1 month, shaking occasionally. Strain into a clear bottle and add a clean, fresh branch of tarragon. Seal with a cork and label.

This preserve is best kept in the fridge once opened.

THYME

When people speak of warm breezes scented with wild herbs, they are usually referring to more southern shores than those of Britain. The wild thyme of the hot Mediterranean hillsides has a pungent fierce scent, which is not reproduced in the wild thyme of mossy British banks. Although our native thyme is delightful and far more subtle, the stronger thyme frequently grown in gardens is much more similar to the continental variety. Thyme has been cultivated for centuries for its rich oils, which have great antiseptic properties, and it has been used in remedies for practically everything from indigestion to whooping cough. This is a powerful herb and a mere sprig will go a long way in the kitchen, so it is one of those herbs that are at their best when used in vinegars, jellies and oils.

Thyme Jelly

A small sprig of thyme may be added to the half set jelly as decoration. Infuse more thyme if you prefer a stronger taste. This is a very useful recipe if you have no delicious fruit juices to use as a base. A large handful of finely chopped basil also makes a good jelly.

MAKES 6 X 175G JARS

3 tablespoons fresh thyme

6 tablespoons white malt vinegar

675g white granulated sugar

125ml commercial pectin

6 x 175g sterilised jars (page 44)

Put the thyme into a bowl and cover with 300ml boiling water. Put a plate over the top and leave to infuse for 15 minutes. Strain and add the vinegar, then add enough extra water, if necessary, to ensure that you have 300ml in all. Pour into a large pan and heat gently, adding the sugar and stirring well until it has dissolved. Bring to the boil for 1 minute and stir in the pectin. Boil for a further 2 minutes, stirring and skimming constantly. Allow to cool before potting. Seal and label when cold.

This preserve can be eaten the next day or when cold. It is best kept in the fridge once opened.

HERBS

INDEX

ACKNOWLEDGEMENTS

I would like to acknowledge the support of Mandy Little as my agent of many years and Kay Halsey for making the business of editing a pleasure.

ANBERRY

ORANGES

HOR

TARRAGON

APRICOTS

MARMALADE

DAMSON F

PEAR

GOOSEBERRY

ANANA

BLACK

MARROW

THYME

ONIO

GARLIC

PLUMS

PEACH

EAT

MANDARIN

FENNEL

BLUEBERRY

DATE

LIMES

CABBAGE

PECTIN S

GRAPEFRUIT

LEMON

APPLES

CURRANTS

SAGE

MINT

E

REENGAGE

CHERRY